Fighting Fuzzy Thinking in

# Poker, Gaming, and Life

*By*
David Sklansky

# A product of Two Plus Two Publishing

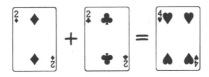

FIRST EDITION

FIRST PRINTING
MAY 1997

*Printing and Binding*
Creel Printing Co.
Las Vegas, Nevada

*Printed in the United States of America*

# POKER, GAMING, AND LIFE
## COPYRIGHT © 1997 DAVID SKLANSKY

For information contact: **Two Plus Two Publishing**
**226 Garfield Dr.**
**Henderson NV 89014**
**(702) 896-1326**

ISBN: 1-880685-17-5

*To My Emily*

# Table of Contents

# About David Sklansky

David Sklansky is generally considered the number one authority on gambling in the world today. Besides his eight books on the subject, David also has produced two videos and numerous writings for various gaming publications. His occasional poker seminars always receive an enthusiastic reception including those given at the Taj Mahal in Atlantic City and the World Series of Poker in Las Vegas.

More recently David has been doing consulting work for casinos, Internet gaming sites, and gaming device companies.

David attributes his standing in the gambling community to three things:

1. The fact that he presents his ideas as simply as possible (sometimes with Mason Malmuth) even though these ideas frequently involve concepts that are deep, subtle, and not to be found elsewhere.

2. The fact that the things he says and writes can be counted on to be accurate.

3. The fact that to this day a large portion of his income is still derived from gambling (usually poker but also occasionally blackjack, sports betting, horses, video games, casino promotions, or casino tournaments).

Thus, those who depend on David's advice know that he still depends on it himself.

### Other Books by David Sklansky
*Hold 'em Poker*
*The Theory of Poker*
*Getting The Best of It*
*Sklansky on Poker*

## Other Books With David Sklansky

*Hold 'em Poker For Advanced Players* by David Sklansky and Mason Malmuth

*Seven-card Stud for Advanced Players* by David Sklansky, Mason Malmuth, and Ray Zee

*Gambling For a Living* by David Sklansky and Mason Malmuth

# Publisher's Note

This volume is a collection of recent articles written by David Sklansky that have appeared in various publications including *Card Player* and *Poker World* magazines. A few have never before appeared in print.

Most of the articles are about poker or gambling. However, David has recently branched out into other areas that lend themselves to his unique style of analysis. Whether the essays are about gambling or not, you will invariably find that almost all of David's writings share three traits:

1. His explanations are simple to understand even when the subject is complex.
2. He addresses issues that are usually misunderstood by most people, even many so called "authorities" (hence the subtitle "Fighting Fuzzy Thinking").
3. His arguments and thus his conclusions are almost irrefutable.

By insisting that his writings meet these criteria David usually achieves his goal of giving his readers the "aha" experience. By this we mean the experience of saying to yourself "Aha, that's true. And it's not that hard to understand. I'm surprised I never thought of that myself." We at Two Plus Two Publishing will be surprised if this book doesn't give you that experience many times over.

# Part One

# Poker and Gaming

# The Four Brothers

Once upon a time, there were four retired brothers who lived together in Las Vegas. Though they weren't rich, they enjoyed a bit of gambling, especially at craps So, every afternoon, to break up the monotony of their day, the four of them went to a casino and played a little craps — very little. They always bet on the pass line, never took odds, and usually played at different tables. Each brother, however, had his own particular betting strategy which he followed religiously.

Brother A always bet $1 on the pass line and would make this dollar bet exactly three times, after which he would always quit, wait for his brothers, and go home.

Brother B also bet $1 on the pass line three times, but unlike Brother A, he would sometimes bet a fourth dollar, but only if he won his first three bets. After that, he would quit.

Brother C was slightly more daring. He also would bet $1 three times, but if he won all three of those bets, he would make a fourth and last bet of $2.

Finally, there was Brother D who was really the rambunctious one. He also would start with three $1 pass line bets and would quit if he lost even one of them, but if he did win all three, he was off to the races. His fourth bet was $2 (like Brother C), but if he won that, he would bet $3, and if he won that, he would bet $4, and so on. He, in other words, would keep increasing his bet by $1 until he finally lost — then he would quit.

After the brothers were done with their afternoon gambling spree, they would all go home together (occasionally, Brother A would have to wait around awhile for the others to get done) and compare notes. They all kept meticulous notes. Then, one day about 10 years after they started their excursions, they sat down to see exactly how each of them was doing at the craps table for that total period of time.

Now, the above story was, of course, fiction, but let's pretend it wasn't. And if it wasn't, there is no doubt as to which of the brothers should be doing the best, the next best, the next best, and the worst, after 10 years. Can you tell me what this order is?

Before I tell you the answer, I'd like to review the question to make sure it is clear. Notice that Brother A (who bets $1, $1, $1) will always go home somewhere between a $3 loser and a $3 winner. Brother B (who bets $1, $1, $1, and sometimes $1) is somewhere between a $3 loser and a $4 winner. Brother C (who bets $1, $1, $1, and sometimes $2) quits somewhere between a $3 loser and a $5 winner. Finally, Brother D (who bets $1, $1, $1, and sometimes $2, and sometimes $3, and sometimes $4, and so on) will wind up between a $3 loser and a who-knows-how-much winner.

So, who will do the best and who will do the worst? Here's a hint. It doesn't matter if the brothers are playing at the same table or not. If you assume they are playing at the same table at the same time, the answer may come easier.

OK, what's the answer? First of all, you should realize that all of the brothers almost certainly are losing after 10 years. The pass line has a 1.4 percent disadvantage, and even Brother A has bet more than $10,000 during this time and figures to be down about $150. But I have just given you the answer! Each brother's expected loss is simply 1.4 percent of their total action. That means that Brother A figures to lose the least, followed by Brother B, then Brother C, with Brother D doing the worst. It's that simple. While it is true that Brother D occasionally will get lucky and beat the others during a 10 year period, it is more likely that he will do worse.

For skeptics, we can show this principle in another way by comparing Brother A and Brother B when they are playing at the same table at the same time. Most days, they do exactly the same, since they usually don't win all three bets But what happens on a day they do? Brother A quits a $3 winner. Brother B plays one more dollar and thus quits either $2 or $4 ahead. However, since he wins this last bet only about 49.3 percent of the time, he will wind up with $2 rather than $4 slightly more often, and his average profit on these days will be slightly less than $3, compared with the $3 profit for Brother A. Similar calculations could be done to show that Brothers C and D do worse yet. However, they are not really necessary. All that you really need to know is that the more money you put into action with a fixed amount the worst of it, the more you eventually will lose. Manipulating your daily result can't change that. In this example, Brother D's maximum daily loss is the same as Brother A's, and his possible win is so much greater. Yet, his overall result will be worse.

What is the bottom line of all this? Why did I choose to start off with a craps example in a book that is mostly about poker? It is because I'm hoping that this story finally will put to rest most of the fallacious ideas about "money management."

Money management is a consideration only when two things are occurring: You have the best of it, and you have a short bankroll that is in danger of being lost by temporary fluctuations. When this situation occurs, it may be correct to quit even though you have the best of it, and you can call that money management. However, it can never be right to quit with the best of it if you have an adequate bankroll, simply because of how you are doing at the time. And it can never be right to play with the worst of it regardless of your bankroll, simply because of how you are doing at the time (except for psychological or entertainment reasons, of course).

Getting back to the brothers for a moment, if these guys had found a game in which they had the best of it (maybe a private craps game in which they could bet don't pass and nothing was barred), then everything would be different. The order would reverse. They all would now win and Brother D would win the most. Why? Simply because he put in the most action with the best of it. The specifics of his daily strategy again would not matter, just the total amount he bet.

# Being a Favorite

When you sit down at a poker game, it isn't enough to simply say to yourself, "I'm a very good player, therefore I should win."

You had better be able to look at the game and say exactly why you'll be able to beat it. In other words, what is it about this game with this structure and these players that makes it profitable for you?

Just being a good player may not be enough to make you a favorite in the game. There are three main possible reasons for this:

1. The other players are also good players.
2. The rake or time take out is high enough to negate your edge.
3. The other players' weaknesses or your strengths can't be taken advantage of in a game with this particular structure.

It is this third character that I want to explore further. It is important to realize that when you name a game and a structure you are also naming a general best strategy to play the game. For instance, if you sit down in an Omaha game with a small ante and a large opening bet, you should know immediately that this requires a tight opening strategy but not so tight once you enter a pot, and almost no bluffing. You should also know that the ability to read the other players' hands is not as important in this game as it is in others. That being the case, you should realize that you can't have much of an edge in this game unless your opponents are loose or bluffing type players. Though players who are very tight and never bluff are basically poor players, you would much prefer to be playing some other game with them.

Lowball draw offers a similar example. Here the main requirements are to know how good a hand to open or call with in various positions before the draw, and to know which hands to bet for value or bluff with after the draw. It is a very straightforward game, almost like blackjack, that requires little ability to read hands, or advanced poker insight.

This is why you will find so many players without very much real poker talent holding their own in the big lowball games in California. In fact, since knowing this straight forward strategy along with having the discipline not to "steam" is the main key to beating lowball, world-class poker players from Las Vegas with great imagination and insight nevertheless usually find themselves getting beat when they tackle these games. Their talents have been wasted.

We can see, then, that if you truly are a world-class player, you should try to find games that will reward your talents. This basically means fairly complicated games with good opportunities for bluffing or other plays. Check raising should be allowed. (It isn't allowed, by the way, in most California lowball games.)

Reading hands should be important. The ante should also be fairly large, though not outlandish. Not only does a large ante punish the tight but weak player, it also allows you to play more hands. As a world-class player, the more hands you can legitimately play without being out of line for the structure, the more opportunity you have to use your greater talents later on in the hand.

However, most of you are not world class players. If you are a winner, it is probably mainly because you have patience and discipline. This is fine, as long as you recognize that fact. Once you recognize it, you will stick to games that reward these attributes. This mainly means a low ante game where many of the other players are playing too loose.

You won't get famous, but you still might get rich.

# The Ability to Play Expertly

My writings have always stressed that the most important aspect of making money at poker is the ability to play expertly. Other factors such as game selection, money management, staying off tilt, etc... are of only secondary importance except in extreme situations.

To illustrate the point in yet another way, I will use as an example two mythical characters, Bob and Joe, who both hit Vegas with a $1,000 gambling bankroll plus expense money. Both of these guys are very good players. They both beat the games they play even though it is hard enough just to break even with the rake and the tough competition. Bob, however, plays slightly better than Joe. His hourly winning rate is one big bet per hour (i.e. $10 per hour in a $5-$10 game, $30 per hour in a $15-$30 game, etc...), but Joe's hourly rate is only about half of that.

There is a principle of mathematics that says that the higher your hourly rate, the less bankroll you need in order to have a small risk of going broke. For Bob, $1,000 ought to be enough to play $5-$10, but Joe would need about $2,000 to give himself an equally safe cushion.[1] Joe is therefore forced to play $2-$4 or $3-$6. He will be averaging $2.50 an hour while Bob makes $10 per hour. Thus, if both players gamble prudently on equal bankrolls, Bob makes not twice as much but four times as much. And this is not the end of the story.

After 100 hours Bob figures to have won $1,000 giving him a total bankroll of $2,000. He can now move up to the $10-$20 game. After another 100 hours he should win another $2,000 giving him $4,000 and a bankroll to play $20-$40. The third hundred hours (at

---

[1]See "Is Your Wallet Fat Enough" on page 130.

$40 per hours) doubles him to $8,000, where he now plays $40-$80 and after 400 hours Bob should have $16,000.[2]

Meanwhile, during the same 400 hours, Joe is earning only $2.50 per hour which means he needs all this time to turn his $1,000 to $2,000. Finally he has the bankroll to play $5-$10 where he can win $5 per hour.

Thus after about 10 weeks of play we find Joe making $5 per hour playing $5-$10 while Bob makes $160 per hour playing $80-$160. What started out as Bob making twice as much as Joe quickly turns into Bob making 32 times as much as Joe.

Admittedly, this example is highly oversimplified. I have not taken expenses into account or the fact that bigger games tend to be tougher. However, these factors usually make it even worse for the slightly less skillful player.

Now the multiplier effect would not be relevant if the lesser player had a very large bankroll. In this case he could simply play just as high as the better player and settle for half the payoff. However, this is not the way it usually is. Most poker players start off with a limited bankroll and try to build it up. In this case the effect just described is quite accurate.

Those players who play just a little bit better than their colleagues will find that their slightly higher win rate (maybe only 20 percent higher) and their slightly lower bankroll requirements will, as time goes by, result in a much bigger bankroll and playing in much bigger games.

Players out there who wonder why some of the world class players are doing so much better than you when they only play a little bit better than you do should think about what I'm saying. And

---

[2]This example is somewhat contrived. First, because the players usually get tougher as you move up in stakes your win rates will not usually double when you go to a game twice as large. Second, you need much more money to play in games as large as $40-$80 than this example shows. However, it still illustrates the point that I am trying to make.

the same goes for those of you who don't think it's worth putting in all the work and thought necessary to be as good as you can.

# Are Great Players Born?

Are great poker players born or made? Can studying poker books and articles make a less talented individual a better player than someone with great instinctive poker ability who cannot or will not read and study? The fact that you are reading this essay obviously says that you think you can improve your game by reading — not just by practice and experience. Thus you probably want the answer to the above question to be that poker players can be "made." And that is the answer. If I didn't think so I wouldn't be writing.

The fact is that many winning players with no particular card talent have approached me to say that my books and writings have been a large factor in their success. On the other hand, I've seen lots of talented individuals, who have stubbornly refused to learn fundamentals via the written word, go broke and stay broke. Now there are of course a few poker players who are both very talented and very studious. Many of the world class players are in this category.

But what of the 500 or so successful or professional players around the country who while not being champions, make good money from poker (in games up to $75-$150)? Why are so many of these winning players not students of the game? Why in other words are there all these players out there who know less than you do, yet seem to do better than you? Let me address this question in detail.

Of the 500 best poker players in the world I would estimate that about half of them have gotten to that point more from reading than from instinct, practice, and experience. Furthermore this number is constantly increasing. Even ten years ago more than 400 of the top 500 were "seat of the pants" players. But in the last ten years two things have happened:

1. Better, more accurate information has been published
2. Less stigma on gambling has resulted in more college types taking up poker

However in spite of this, about half of the best players do little or no studying. There are a few reasons for this and if *you* are in the studious group it could be helpful to your success as a poker player if you understood them.

First of all is the simple concept of evolution or survival of the fittest. Players who mathematically analyze which hands are worth playing and how to play them (or who go by authors who do this analysis for them) would seem to have an advantage over those who don't make this effort. And they do. However a certain small percentage of non-studious players will hit upon the approximate correct strategy to a particular game basically by chance. And they are the ones that survive! The vast majority of the non-studious players have gone broke well before making their way to the $20-$40 game that you are playing in. You only meet up with those few who have great talent or more likely just so happen to have hit upon a decent strategy.

To illustrate this concept with numbers, I contend that no more than one percent of those who try to make it as a poker player without serious studying succeed. On the other hand I think that about 10 percent of good students succeed. But since the first group is so much larger than the second group (say 25,000 vs. 2,500) we wind up with about equal numbers of successful players from each group. (However the successful players from the non-studying group almost invariably play only one game well. This should be expected since they probably just fell into a correct strategy by chance rather than by understanding the underlying general theory of poker that would help them play many games well. The theoretically grounded player is far more likely to be able to beat two or more different games. More on this later.) So we see that those who study poker writings are far more likely to succeed. Still the fact is that just being studious does not guarantee success.

Probably 90 percent of poker students are only small winners, break even, or small losing players. This is not as bad as the 99 percent or so of aspiring players who fail, who are not students, but it is still awfully high. Knowing why this is so may be the key to your own improvement. So here are the reasons:

**A. Not everything you read is correct.** Before 1976 virtually everything you could read about poker had major errors in it. The stuff was just wrong. If you followed the written advice you were destined to lose in any semi-tough game. Nowadays it is not as bad with much written poker information being right on the money. But a lot isn't. To write a book or article on medicine or building bridges you have to have the proper credentials. And the editors of most academic journals are experts themselves who can evaluate the accuracy of articles submitted to them. This has never been true of poker publications. I have read many poker articles written by mediocre players or outright incompetents where the advice is simply incorrect. (It is true that correct poker strategy is in some cases sometimes debatable and a matter of opinion. Usually however it is clear cut.)

Of course good poker students can usually pick out these bad writings and ignore them. What is more dangerous in my mind are the half decent player-writers who are usually correct but not always. Now if you religiously follow the advice of a writer who is right 99 percent of the time he will certainly do you more good than harm. But if he's wrong 15 percent of the time, it's another story. Those mistakes could easily cost you more money than his correct advice makes you. (Ironically the players who adjust their play based on experience rather than by reading are much quicker to change something that doesn't work than the student who thinks he got some good advice from a so called expert.)

The question of course is which writings can you trust to be almost certainly correct. I will not answer that question directly, but will instead suggest a way that you can find out for yourself. Approach ten winning players who you know got to be winner mainly via reading. If they won't lie to you, ask them what they have read and studied. Ignore anything not mentioned by at least eight of them.

**B. Some readers underrate experience.** I'm sorry to say that there are many players who religiously study my books without realizing that those books cannot cover every situation that can arise in a poker game. Egghead types who try to learn poker in the same way as they might learn blackjack are probably destined to fail. When someone tells me that they have totally memorized my list of starting hands for hold 'em, I cringe.

**C. You need a moderate amount of talent and/or brains.** I wish that everyone who paid good money for my books and studied them religiously was destined to win. But it is clear to me that that is not the case. Just as a person with little athletic ability can never be a great golfer merely by learning the mechanics of the game, the same is probably true for the studious person with no innate card sense. This problem can occasionally be overcome by a student with a very high IQ but we don't all possess that.

**D. Some students have no discipline.** This of course is a problem for students and non-students alike. In fact it should be less of a problem for the analytical player rather than the seat of the pants player as he supposedly understands the concept of independent events. Nevertheless there are those players who know full well how to play right (e.g. throw bad hands away) but cannot bring themselves to do it.

**E. Books can't help much with no-limit, shorthanded, or very tough games.** The vast majority of professional poker players make their living by playing in fairly easy limit "ring" games. It is in these games that having the fundamentals is so important. Intricate psychological ploys are rarely employed. However the very biggest games are frequently not in this category. The well known world class high rolling poker players are often playing in shorthanded games against very good opponents. Sometimes they are playing no-limit or pot limit. The right strategy for these games is many times a lot different than the right strategy for the more typical game. Good books do get into the psychology and game theory that can be used in these tough games, but it is impossible to go into all the detail that is necessary.

So what sometimes happens is that a poker player who has been winning a lot of money in the medium size games by using the fundamental strategies he has so diligently studied, tries to get rich quick in one of these big tough shorthanded games. A few student types have succeeded, but most don't.

**F. Theoretical students should diversify rather than play specialists at their own game.** While many of my books are on one game only, the one I am most proud of is *The Theory of Poker*. This is the book that explains concepts that apply to almost any type of poker game. It shows you how to think about poker situations rather than just what to do. Thus, those of you who study this book carefully are well on their way to playing many different games well. And if you do, it is silly to give away that advantage by sticking to only one game. As mentioned before, non-studious players usually have no choice but to play only one game as this is the game where they fell into the right strategy. (Even that game would probably give them trouble if you changed the structure on them.) You on the other hand can play all games well. Therefore, your proper battle plan is to pick the easiest game available regardless if it is stud, Omaha, hold 'em or whatever. Let the specialist who doesn't understand poker in general be your unpaid shills rather than play into their hands. (Either do that or play in games where more than one variation is dealt.) Failure to heed this advice is yet another reason why some poker students fail.

**G. Reading books is different from reading hands.** We now come to what I think is the biggest factor explaining why a few talented, non-studious players surpass almost all the bookworms. It is the fact that books cannot by themselves make you an expert at reading other player's hands. On the other hand, some talented players do become great hand readers simply through experience. And reading hands well can easily be your strongest weapon. (To take this point to the extreme, imagine you were using "marked cards" and thus knew what all your opponents had. You would certainly be able to destroy this game even without knowing any advanced poker theory. A great card reader is, to a lessor extent, in this same situation. Some books do try to give you a guideline as to how to read hands. My books show how logical deduction can frequently narrow down an opponent's holding based on the way he played his hand on previous betting rounds as well as the present one. While this method can be quite accurate, it frankly takes a talented mind to be able to do it in the heat of battle. It also assumes that your opponent is playing rationally (and is starting off within a certain group of predictable hands. This is another reason why it is easier to learn how to play ring games as opposed to shorthanded games from a book. Your opponent's possible starting hands are easier to surmise.) When your opponent is playing in a tricky or irrational way however, logical deduction won't help you read his hand. But there are talented players who can do this even if they don't read a book. Their gift is their power of observation.

The edge an observant player has over a merely studious player is that the observant player will be better able to adjust his play depending on who he is playing against. He will adjust depending on what he has observed in the past and how he thinks that will affect the future. (Actually this *could* be explained fairly well via the written word. Perhaps I will get to it someday.)

The observant player will also be better able to pick up opponents "tells." Some players sometimes have physical mannerisms that tend to give away their hands. But each player is different. The same mannerism that may indicate a weak hand in one player may indicate a strong hand in another. And this can only be picked out by careful observation. (The problem with books on tells is that though they can give some good guidelines, the tells cited are not true for all players. Worse yet, is the fact that if your opponent has also read the book he might purposely reverse things on you which [if you are not careful] will make it more costly than if *you* had never read the book yourself.)

Again, I stress that you can't become a great poker player if you try to play and learn it like it was blackjack.

**H. Many "by the book" players don't preplan fancy options.**
There is a way for the studious non-talented player to negate much of the disadvantage he has against his more imaginative and creative opposition. Since he knows he can't think as quickly as them in the heat of battle, the idea is to think out *categories* of creative plays well in advance, so that they become automatic during the game. You can either read about them or think them up yourself. Here are some examples:

> **1. Hold 'em** — A tough player raises, everyone else folds, and you who are the big blind calls with

The flop comes

You check and call. Fourth street is the

You check and he checks behind you. The last card is the

The play is to go for a check raise! Space doesn't permit an analysis of this play, but good players should see the reasons. The idea is to think about situations of this type before they come up so that you make the play automatically.

**2. Hold 'em** — You have been checking and calling all the way with a flush draw and an inside straight draw. In general you should know beforehand that you will bet right out if the flush card comes but go for a check raise if the straight card comes (unless that straight card becomes the highest card on board.) Again preplan this. Don't deduce it at the table.

**3. Seven-card stud** — You have a pair of jacks, the player to your left apparently has a higher pair, and the player to your right with a small open pair comes out betting. If it is fifth street or sixth street the play is to raise if you think the bettor has only two small pair below jacks up. Once again there are many variations on this theme and you should ponder them *before* you play.

So you see that the bottom line is that there are some very good reasons why there are winning players who don't have all the technical information about poker and losing players who do. On the other hand, I hope this essay has given my readers some hints as to how to narrow any talent gap they may have with these "brilliant illiterates." In most cases if you follow my advice that gap will have become so small that your superior knowledge will now in fact make you the superior player.

# Talent Versus Discipline

What does it take to be a professional poker player? This question has been taken up by other writers but never by me. Now I, (a real life professional player) want to give it a shot.

I am constantly frustrated by the questions that are asked of me, whether they be by private students, at my seminars, or merely by someone who asks me for a minute of my time. I am frustrated because the questions are so often unrelated to the subjects that really matter when it comes to being a great poker player. (And if you want to be a professional player in a public cardroom, you have to be a great player, not just a good one. The rake and the quality of your opponents demand it.

The problem is that even fairly decent players ask the wrong questions. These usually involve things like knowing when to quit a game, when to push their "rush," what bankroll they need for a particular stakes, etc... However, these things are of little or no importance and in fact are completely irrelevant, if the player is not a favorite in the game! In other words, you must play the game extremely well before any of the above questions matter, and if you do play extremely well they won't matter much.

My friend and colleague Mike Caro likes to lecture on taking advantage of your image at the table. This can be an important feature of your game. So are the "tells" which he is an authority on. The only thing that bothers me when I attend his lectures is that once again many of the students want to learn these concepts without first learning how to play excellently. This is a shame because Mike's stuff can be profitable, if you are a favorite in the game, but not otherwise. But people, unfortunately, would rather read novels than textbooks.

Thus, the main attribute of a great player is to have tremendous knowledge of the game. This includes the logic, the math, and the psychology, and knowing how to intertwine them. This shouldn't surprise you. The same is true for backgammon, chess, and bridge. Why should it be any different for poker?

There are, however, two other important attributes of the great poker player. One is simply talent. By this, I basically mean the ability to think fast in the heat of battle and the ability to instantly adjust as the situation changes. Talent is, of course, far more important for those playing hold 'em and stud, where some cards are showing and there are several betting rounds. Playing draw and lowball, you mainly need knowledge.

Is there any way to acquire this talent if you're not born with it? I don't think so, but there is another alternative: Study and think about the game so long and hard that almost any situation which can arise in a game has already been considered. Now you can use knowledge to handle a situation where others need talent.

There is one other attribute that is essential. It is discipline. I once knew someone who had all the talent in the world. This person also had no trouble with the knowledge. One hour after learning BASIC language for the computer, he programmed the Fibonacci sequence. However, he couldn't handle a loss at poker and is now a mailman in Des Moines.

In my writings, I usually don't even mention discipline. That's because with me it goes without saying. However, I may take too much for granted. So many otherwise good players don't make it because they play badly when losing. The basic problem is that they can't be content with getting just a portion of their loss back for that session. They can't psychologically think of all games as one big poker game and that tomorrow is another day. They want to go to sleep a winner, and if they don't, how much they lose doesn't matter.

For those of you who have this problem a little will power wouldn't hurt. Hopefully the following chapter will help you get it.

# Will Power

It is often thought that one of the main reasons for my success as a poker player is the fact that I don't steam or "go on tilt" when I am losing. In point of fact, the ability to keep from steaming is not nearly as important as the ability to choose games and play well. It is true, however, that you must do better in the long run if you are always playing your best and choosing good games, regardless of whether you are winning or losing. Despite this obvious fact, not steaming is easier said than done. So, how do I do it?

It is important to understand that playing your best or quitting a bad game when you are stuck actually is an act of will power, the same kind of will power that you need to stay on a diet, quit smoking, or start an exercise program. What is happening in all these cases is that you are trying to put up with some discomfort today in order to gain even greater rewards in the future. In the case of poker playing, the discomfort is the bad feeling that you get when you go home a loser that evening. The only way to have a chance at alleviating that feeling when you are badly stuck is to play a lot of hands that you shouldn't play, in a desperate attempt to get even for the day. That strategy will usually backfire, of course, but occasionally it works. If you play your normal, solid game, you can hope to recoup only a portion of your losses, and the bad feeling remains.

Of course, getting back some of your losses adds that much more to your eventual profits, if you are a winning player. Since the ability to accept the lousy feeling of a sure loss today for even greater rewards in the future is a mark of will power, we see that not steaming is, in fact, a test of will power.

I have come up with a few techniques to develop my own will power. They ought to work for you, also. First, l realized that there is a big difference between thoughts and feelings, and in the short run, feelings take precedence. Therefore, my idea was to make my feelings rather than my thoughts give me will power.

One way to harness your feelings to give yourself will power is to take great *pride* when you stick to a resolution, and to feel great *shame* when you don't. Make yourself feel that sticking to your resolution is more important than the subject matter of that resolution. If you can develop this attitude, you will have will power without having to resort to logic to talk yourself into playing well or exercising. You do it because it feels worse if you don't. *Make yourself feel more pain from letting yourself down than the pain you feel by exercising or losing, and your emotions will keep you on the right course, automatically.*

A second way to harness your own emotions to give your will power strength is to realize that time is merely a dimension. Physics tells us that, and it's true. Time is just another way of specifying where we are. If I gave you $1 million and, simultaneously, transported you to Australia, you would still be happy in spite of your changed location. You should feel the same about time.

Three months from now, you would rather have $67,000 than $65,000, even if it meant one extra losing day three months earlier. Six months from now, you would rather be thin than fat, even if it meant some hungry days leading up to it. So the key to this technique is to think of the rewards of your will power not occurring in the future, but simply at another place. (The only drawback to this way of looking at things involves incidents from your past. For those incidents that were good, this philosophy makes it easier to relive and savor them. However, when they were bad, or when someone has wronged you, it is not true that "time heals all wounds." It would make no more sense to forgive someone who has made no amends, simply because four years have gone by, than it would to forgive him the next day simply because he moved to Australia.)

Anyway, time is only a dimension, and the ability to visualize your greater happiness in the future, just as if it were happening in another place, cannot fail to help your will power to do the right thing.

Note: This essay is also in the "Life" section of this book.

# A Comment on Poker Books

I would like to address the general concept of learning about poker simply from reading. It is no secret that many successful players have learned little or nothing from poker books or articles. This includes some champion players. However, that doesn't mean that reading about poker is of little value. The fact is that many of the superstars are freaks. They have an inborn talent for the game as most champion athletes do. It is safe to assume that most readers do not have this talent. They thus cannot hope to achieve top level play without a lot of help. (However you might be surprised at how many of the world class players *have* read many works on poker and how many of them have told me that they picked up a thing or two from my books.)

Another reason why many poker champions have learned their trade exclusively from experience rather than reading is that until relatively recently, few books were worthwhile. They frequently contained enough misinformation to do more harm than good. No wonder the best players didn't get that way from reading. If you followed the advice in many books you would find yourself a mediocre, easy to read player. You would have little chance against even a semi-pro.

However things have changed. Now that professional players rather than professional writers have put their ideas in print, very valuable information can be learned just from reading.

Being good at poker is something like being good at bowling or golf. You need talent to become a superstar no matter how much you know. However with proper coaching, practice, and study most people should be able to achieve one notch below superstar status. Most people can become 190 bowlers or shoot 77 in golf if they have a coach who can show them all the fundamentals. It is not necessary that they have that much talent. With proper coaching, practice, and study  they can frequently surpass people who have much more talent but who don't want to study and practice the fundamentals.

Thus, I would like you to consider me your poker coach. I might only be able to get you to be a 77 shooter but this is good enough. Even if you can't get on the pro tour with this score, there is plenty of money to be made if you're this good. This is especially true in poker. There are a lot of 90 shooters out there just waiting to give you their money. Let me help you take it.

# For the Studious Player

The fact that you are reading this book tells me that you are probably a serious player who wants to learn all he or she can to improve his or her game. Unfortunately, it also tells me that you are probably not a world-class superstar.

The fact is that there are a chosen few who simply have such extraordinary instinct and talent for poker that they don't have to study the fundamentals, as you do, in order to be extremely successful.

However, it is because of the existence of these few poker "freaks" that gives many players the mistaken idea that they also can be successful without learning the game in a scholarly manner. Without the same innate talent you cannot expect to duplicate the results of these few uneducated superstars. On the contrary, those who try are almost certainly doomed to failure.

You, on the other hand, as a serious student of the game can almost guarantee yourself a successful poker career without any inborn "card sense." Study and hard work make up for all but the greatest talent. Sometimes it does even more than that.

While it is true that untalented, studious players can expect to lose against great intuitive players, that is only true because they are playing the intuitive player's best game. Had they changed the game, changed the rules, or changed the structure, the expert poker student could well become the favorite.

Changing the game or playing dealer's choice as they do in home games favors those who know poker theory and hurts those who rely mainly on experience. In fact, even if you are not playing dealer's choice, you have a good chance to beat the merely talented but uneducated player, if you pick the right game. Conversely, there are some games where you would be at a big disadvantage. The question thus becomes, what is the best game for the player who works hard on study and practice but who may not have the talent or experience to make quick decisions in the heat of battle. For this type of player I will list ten poker games from best to worst:

**1. Lowball draw.** You can play the game almost perfectly by using the correct memorized strategy. Even bluffing situations can be handled well by using a randomizing strategy that also can be memorized.

**2. Seven-card stud hi-lo split with no qualifier.** If you play like I say in Doyle Brunson's book, you will beat all but the best.

**3. Seven-card razz.** The razz section in my book *Sklansky on Poker* covers almost all possible situations. The times that you need card sense or expert psychological ability are rare.

**4. Pot Limit Omaha.** While the intuitive player frequently can make big wins at the game, the solid player will almost always grind out a small profit in all but the toughest games.

**5. Jacks or better draw.** While a memorized strategy should keep you about even, the real profit comes from expert play after the draw, which is hard to learn from a book.

**6. California draw.** Opening strategies are mathematical, but from then on there are lots of opportunities for imagination.

**7. Seven-card stud hi-lo split eight-or-better.** Sometimes this game reverts to regular hi-lo strategy. More often you encounter complex situations that have to be evaluated on the spur of the moment.

**8. Limit hold 'em.** Only the first round is fairly automatic. From then on there is plenty of room for insightful play.

**9. Seven-card stud.** This is a complex game made even more complex by the necessity of remembering the cards that have been folded, and knowing how to adjust based on this information. Knowledge of the game is important, but it is far from everything.

**10. No-limit hold 'em.** This is the hardest game to learn from a book. Experience and instinct play too large a role, especially when the game is shorthanded.

One last point. If as part of your study you have learned to discipline yourself to play your best even when losing, you have yet another advantage over some "superstars" that may well make you the favorite even at their best game.

# Sizing Up Those Flashes

Every year two or three new players take the poker world by storm. They come from nowhere and seem to win almost all the money, sometimes even in the biggest games. This goes on for months. However, very few of them are around three years later, and those that are, are frequently just breaking even, living off the money they accumulated in their early wins. What happens to them? Is it drugs? Are they being cheated? Do they simply lose their intensity? Surely it couldn't be that they were bad players who just started out lucky and now there luck has run out. After all, there is no way a bad player can win for months.

To explain this phenomenon you must first realize that there are literally thousands of people every year who try to become professional poker players in the legalized cardrooms of Nevada, California, New Jersey, Connecticut, Arizona, Mississippi, Washington, and elsewhere. Most don't have a chance. There are however a couple of hundred who are break even players or small favorites. Now consider 100 people flipping five coins each. Three of them should get all heads. If it wasn't so obvious that coin flipping is all luck, these three people might think they each have a talent, instead of realizing that they were simply one of those three out of 100 that figured to succeed in getting five heads.

This is exactly what happens in the poker world. For instance, a pro in the $30-$60 seven-card stud game in Vegas could find his income varying by as much as $50,000 in either direction for one year simply because of chance alone. If his average year is $80,000, he might fall to $30,000 or might make $130,000. The extremes should occur about two or three percent of the time. Thus, if you have a group of 100 players who figure to break even or win a little for the year, two or three of them will win $50,000 by chance alone. This is especially true for those players who play a fast aggressive game. Since their standard deviation is higher, it is easier for them to get temporarily lucky even though their ultimate results will be in the break-even range.

The technical name for this concept is Regression to the Mean. It is the real explanation, for instance, of the so-called Sophomore Slump in professional sports, where the Rookie of the Year invariably has a lesser second year than his first. (It also explains many other things that I won't go into here.)

The main thing to keep in mind is that you can't really judge a poker player until he's proved himself for a few years. Be especially skeptical about these new young super-aggressive players who play their highly fluctuating game. And don't get too cocky if you're one of them. I've seen about 100 of them come — and about 90 of them go.

# Paying For Information

Suppose that while you are playing blackjack for $100 a hand, the dealer offers to flash his hole card on the upcoming deal if you give him a big enough tip right now. What is the most that you can give him and still make this a good deal for you? It may surprise you that even if you take ultimate advantage of this situation (take insurance, hit 19 or 20 if necessary, splits tens, and so on), you can't pay more than about $12 for this information. If you were to pay, say, $15 per $100 bet, you would lose more in the long run than if you played your normal game. Even $12 would be too much to pay if there is the slightest chance that you could misread the flashed card. A little reflection ought to help you see why this is so. For one thing, many of your decisions will not change even if you know his hole card. For instance, if you are dealt 19 and his upcard is eight or less, you would stand whether you knew his hole card or not. If you are dealt 14 and the dishonest dealer shows his ten in the hole with his six upcard, you will stand just as you would if you hadn't seen his card. Furthermore, it frequently can occur that even though you change your strategy because you know that his hole card does, it does you no good, and may even cost you money.

When the dealer has 20, your hitting 18 rather than standing as usual will rarely help. When you stand on 15 because the dealer has a nine showing and a six in the hole, your revised strategy easily can cost you $200 when the next card is a baby and you turn what would have been your $100 win into a $100 loss. ("Wise-guy" double downs in this situation, while profitable in the long run, sometimes may cost $300 — when you lose $200 while the "ignorant" play would have won $100.) So you can see that even obviously important information, such as what is the blackjack dealer's hole card, is not as valuable as it might appear when you take into account that it often will not help you, and sometimes will even hurt you. If you add to this the possibility that the information might not be 100 percent accurate, it is worth less still.

One of the plays that some experienced poker players make is to bet or raise early with certain mediocre hands in order to "find out" what they are up against. The rationale is that if their opponent raises or reraises, they can dump their hand early. This saves future bets that they would have had to put into the pot had they not solidified their information by putting in an extra bet or two in the earlier round. So, in essence, they are "paying" for information much as in the blackjack example. But are they paying too much? In general, I think they are, and the reasons are analogous to what we said concerning blackjack holecard information.

When determining how much information is worth (and, therefore, what is the most that we can pay for it), we must know four factors. They are:

1. What are the chances that the information is accurate?
2. What are the chances that the information is different than what we already assumed?
3. How often will changing your original assumption also change your decisions or strategy?
4. How much do you gain, on average, when you do change your strategy based on your newfound information?

Let's look at these factors one at a time.

If we are talking about poker, factor No. 1 can be of enormous significance. This is because your opponent is under no obligation to give you accurate information even if you "pay" for it. In other words, when you raise him, he may reraise without having a strong hand, or just call when he does. Against players like this, risking extra money to gain information is usually just stupid.

Factor No. 2 can be very important, but is frequently underestimated or overlooked. The thing to understand is that it does you no good to learn information if you already were assuming that the information was true. So, if someone who has just checked out all the cardrooms in Las Vegas offers to tell me where the best game is for $200, I have wasted my money if he tells me that it is at the Horseshoe and I was going there anyway. In other words, the more likely that the information simply will confirm your original opinion, the less it is worth.

Now, even if you do get information that you did not expect, it means nothing if this new, surprising information does not change your strategy. This is factor No. 3. In poker, it would mean that it is silly to risk extra money to find out that your opponent has a strong hand if your hand has a reasonable chance to draw out on him, and, thus, you must keep on playing anyway. (So, ironically, the few times that the play may be right is when you have few or no outs, rather than when you do have outs. For example, if the flop in hold 'em is

an extra raise early with

may be smarter than with

against a player who will give away whether or not he has flopped a flush.)

Finally, even if you have gotten accurate information that changes your opinion and changes your play, this information still may not be all that valuable. It isn't if the new play that you will now make doesn't increase your mathematical expectation that much. If my Vegas informant had steered me to cardroom B instead of to cardroom A, his $200 fee was still exorbitant if the game there was worth only $20 more per hour than games elsewhere. If, because I find out that the dealer has 17, I don't double down on 11, I gain only just a little. These are two examples of factor No. 4.

It is important to understand that the concepts just discussed regarding the value or fair price for information apply to any decision-making situation, not just gambling. Furthermore, the four factors that go into this can be quite precisely used and related in an algebraic formula. But I have spared you for now.

# The Importance of Position

An important concept that all expert poker players know is that your position in the sequence of betting may reduce the pot odds you are getting. If a player ahead of you bets and there is a possible raise to your left, you must be cognizant of the fact that that possibility cuts down your odds. If for example, there is a $100 pot and the bet is $20, you appear to be getting 6-to-1 odds ($120-to-$20). However, when there is a raiser behind you and the original bettor calls, you are really getting only 4½-to-1 if you call the raise. Although the pot has grown to $180, you must put in a total of $40. If the original bettor reraises, your odds drop to 3⅔-to-1. The pot grows to $220 (assuming the opponent behind you calls the reraise), but you have to put in $60. What's more, your chances of winning, even when you make your hand, have certainly decreased with all that raising going on between your opponents, suggesting they have pretty big hands.

How does the concept of position vis-á-vis pot odds work in practice?

Let's say in seven-card stud you have a four flush in six cards and a player to your right bets after pairing his *door card.* (The door card is the first open card the player receives. When it is paired on board, *trips,* or three-of-a-kind, is a strong possibility since the player may have started with a pair.) At the same time the player with the open pair bets, you notice that a player to your left has caught a card that looks as if it has made him a straight. Before you call the first bet, you must be aware that the player to your left may raise if he made a straight (or even if he didn't). Furthermore, the original bettor may reraise with three-of-a-kind or, of course, a full house. So, before calling the first bet, you have to assess your pot odds not just at the moment, but in the event there is a raise or two behind you. You also have to decide what your chances of winning are if you do make the flush. You would, of course, beat the straight, but the question is whether the original bettor is the kind of player who would bet into a possible straight with less than a full house or at the very least three-of-a-kind.

Adjusting your pot odds before calling a bettor to your right with players behind you comes up most often in games like five-card draw, draw lowball and hold 'em.

Let's say in hold 'em you have the

and the flop comes

You would seem to have a strong hand with the top pair, but if you are in second position with a number of players behind you and the player in first position bets, you should probably throw away your aces. Not only has the player in first position suggested a great deal of strength with his bet, but he may get raised by such hands as an ace-king, ace-queen and three-of-a-kind, which shortens your pot odds and further decreases the possibility of your ending up with the best hand. Additionally, the chance of calls from flush draws and straight draws behind you further diminishes the strength of your pair of aces. You face the uncomfortable double possibility of being second-best at the moment and being out drawn on the last two cards.

Similarly, in seven-card stud you might have to throw away a pair of tens in the hole if the player representing jacks to your immediate right bets.

Not only do you figure to be second-best to the jacks, but someone behind you might raise, thus reducing your pot odds and chances of winning. On the other hand, you'd probably call in a late position, especially because of the deceptive value of your hidden pair.

# Highest On the Flop

Here is an interesting chart I recently worked out that I haven't seen elsewhere. It gives the chances that a particular card will be the highest card in a three card flop.

It can be particularly useful when deciding how to play a medium pair in your hand or when playing against what you think is your opponent's pair.

The probability that the highest card on the flop will be an:

| Card | Percent |
|-------|---------|
| Ace | 21.7 |
| King | 18.3 |
| Queen | 15.2 |
| Jack | 12.4 |
| Ten | 9.9 |
| Nine | 7.6 |
| Eight | 5.7 |
| Seven | 4.0 |
| Six | 2.6 |
| Five | 1.5 |
| Four | 0.74 |
| Trey | 0.24 |
| Deuce | 0.02 |

This chart doesn't take into account the cards in your own hand.

# Dealing Out Hands

There are some serious poker students who don't have computers to do their work. Their method of determining the chances of one hand against another is simply to deal out a thousand or so hands and note the results. Unfortunately, if you do this purely randomly you are apt to get quite inaccurate results. There is, however, a good way to reduce these inaccuracies tremendously. It involves two techniques.

1. Deal through the deck. For instance, if you are dealing cards out to see how

will do against

in seven-card stud, you will deal four cards to each hand and record the winner. But don't return those eight cards to the deck and reshuffle. Instead, deal out the unused portion. This greatly reduces the chances of fluky results (such as the two queens constantly catching a third one).

2. After dealing out the two hands, *reverse them*. In the example just presented after giving four cards to both hands, switch the four cards. This technique is even more effective than the other one in eliminating fluky results — by, for instance, one hand constantly making two pair but not the other one.

These techniques will reduce the number of necessary trial hands by a gigantic amount. In fact, I highly recommend that even those of you who simulate on a computer should use them (as part of the computer) program for even more accurate results.[3]

---

[3]This essay was written before the days of high speed personal computers.

# A Simple Technique

In this essay, I will show you the simplest possible technique to get the exact odds for one hand against another in hold 'em when there are still two cards to come.

Most good poker players can do the problem easily enough when there is only one card to come. They simply count up the number of "wins" for a particular hand and compare this number to the 44 unseen cards (44 = 52 minus the 4 cards in the middle and the 4 cards in both players' hands.) Thus, if one player has two pair and the other has a flush, the two pair's chances of winning with one card to come are simply 4 out of 44 or 1/11 or 10-to-1.

With two cards to come, however, the problem is much more complicated. It's not that hard to figure out the chances of making a hand with various numbers of wins and two tries at it. (However, beware against making the mistake of thinking that "five wins twice" is the same as 10 wins once. It's not.) The hard part is taking into account "backdoor draws" and "redraws." A backdoor draw, for example, would be where a hand that is going for a straight makes a flush instead by catching two consecutive of a particular suit. A redraw occurs when the second best hand draws out on the next to last card, only to be redrawn out on the last card.

In spite of these difficulties I have come up with a method that will result in the absolutely right answer without requiring a computer or painstaking mathematics.

The basic idea behind this technique is to count the number of fifth street winning cards a particular hand will have for every possible fourth street card that can come off, and then take a *weighted average* of the number of fifth street wins (which is then compared to 44). For instance, if a particular hand will have an average of 10 wins with one card to come, its chances are 10/44 or 3.4-to-1.

As an example, let's say Hand 1 is

and Hand 2 is

The flop is

What are the aces chances? You figure thusly:

If fourth street is a deuce, the ace will have two fifth street wins (two aces). If fourth street is a seven, the aces will have zero fifth street wins. If fourth street is a queen, the aces will have four fifth street wins (two aces + two queens). If fourth street is a spade (except the deuce of spades), the aces will have 10 fifth street wins (two aces + eight spades besides the deuce). If fourth street is an ace, the aces will have 43 fifth street wins (anything but a seven). Finally, if fourth street is anything else, the aces will have two fifth street wins (an ace).

To summarize:

> Two fourth street cards give the aces 43 wins
> Three fourth street cards give the aces four wins
> One fourth street card gives the aces no win
> Nine fourth street cards give the aces 10 wins
> 30 fourth street cards give the aces two wins.

This results in a weighted average of a little over 5½ wins on the end. The odds are about 38½-to-5½ or about 7-to-1.

A short cut method that gets you the right price even quicker is to multiply the number of fifth street wins times the number of fourth street cards that would result in that number of wins. In this example:

$$
\begin{aligned}
(2)(3) &= 86 \\
(3)(4) &= 12 \\
(1)(0) &= 0 \\
(9)(10) &= 90 \\
(30)(2) &= 60
\end{aligned}
$$

You then add these results to get 248.

$$248 = 86 + 12 + 0 + 90 + 60$$

This number you put over the figure 1980. The answer is thus 12.53 percent.

$$12.53\% = \left( \frac{248}{1980} \right)(100)$$

The exact odds are 1732-to-248.

$$1732 = 1980 - 248$$

Let us try once more. Hand 1 is

Hand 2 is

and the flop is

You simply set up a table like this:

**Computation for the AK**

| No. Of 4th St. Cards | No. Of 5th St. wins | Product |
|---|---|---|
| 3 (ace) | 40 (everything except eight or seven) | 120 = (3)(40) |
| 2 (king) | 44 (no draws outs) | 88 = (2)(44) |
| 4 (eight or seven) | 2 (king) | 8 = (2)(4) |
| 36 (remaining cards) | 8 (ace or king or running pair) | 288 = (8)(36) |

Adding the product column gives us 504.

$$504 = 120 + 88 + 8 + 288$$

Thus the chances for the ace-king are 504 out of 1980. The odds are 1476-to-504 which is equivalent to 41- to-14 or about 2.9-to-1.

# The Big Excuse

A guy walks up to the craps table with a thousand bucks. He's trying to win himself a hundred dollars and will quit if he does. But he is prepared to risk the whole thousand in quest of that hundred. This guy has been doing this once a week for many years and he wins way more than he loses. He wins about 85 percent of the time. Still, he is down quite a bit for his total play. Now you might say that this fellow is using bad "money management." However, if he was to risk, let's say, only one hundred dollars in his quest for a hundred dollar win, he would win less than half the time. It is only because he sometimes comes back from a large deficit (even eight or nine hundred down) to win his hundred that he has his high percentage of wins.

Before explaining how this anecdote relates to poker players, I want to explain one more point about it. If this man were playing a game where he had the best of it, such as counting blackjack, and still used this win-a-hundred-or-lose-a-thousand strategy, he would have a win loss ratio of above 91 percent, and thus show a long run profit. His money management may be ill advised (why quit with the best of it?) but he would still win. The fact is that any money management scheme will show a long run profit if you are gambling with the best of it and a loss if you aren't.

Now let me tell you about someone else. (Actually, the first person was fictional but this person isn't.) He plays the middle sized poker games in Vegas and wins far more than he loses. If you counted only his wins, his hourly win rate would be about $60. Some catastrophic losses bring it down to about $10. He says his problem is not quitting when he gets moderately stuck. The thing is, he forgets the times when he was moderately stuck, keeps on playing, and winds up winning. If he did quit after a moderate loss he would have no catastrophes, but he would also have a much lower win percentage and therefore approximately the same hourly win rate. It is true that he probably doesn't play as well when he is badly stuck but this can be shown to be a fairly negligible factor as far as long run win rates are concerned.

The point that I am making is that many players try to fool themselves into thinking that their long run disappointing results are not really a true reflection of their money making ability because they feel they can somehow throw out their very bad losses, attributing it to a bad money management decisions that they will not repeat in the future. This is hogwash. As I said, they forget those times that they turned it around to lose less, or even win, as in the dice example. The fact of the matter is that many of the best poker players are known to have the tendency to quit after small or moderate wins but to put in long sessions when they are stuck. Thus, they have the occasional terrible loss. In spite of this, they are big winners. Now I don't advise this method of play. I only say that if you do it, you can't use it as an excuse for your poor long run results. Sometimes I think that a lot of players use this money management scheme of trying to win at all costs just so they can have an excuse to cloud the issue. If they operated differently and more normally they wouldn't do any better, but now they wouldn't have anything to blame it on.

# Steam Games

My regular readers know that I have devoted much of my writing to the importance of not "steaming" or going "on tilt" when you are losing. To achieve good long run results it is imperative that you don't play differently while behind in a desperate attempt to get even for the day. The preaching is over. Some players will never get the message and now I want to show you the best way to punish them.

As always, the serious player should select the best game available when he has a choice. This usually means sitting in a game with a few weak players. However, it can occur that it is worth setting down against normally tough opponents if some of them are losing and are known to be steamers. In fact it may be worth playing against some potential steamers even if they are not yet losing in the hopes that they will take some bad beats that will set them off. However, if you do use this strategy (which I recommend only for experts) you should quit if these potential steamers pull too far ahead.

When trying to decide whether to play in a particular poker game because some normally good players are going on tilt, it is important to take into account exactly what kind of game it is. This is because some games are much more conducive to steaming and will thus more likely get a steamer in trouble than other games. Steamers will play hands that they shouldn't, and overplay their legitimate hands. However, they will not just throw their money away on nearly hopeless hands. For this reason steamers are more likely to "get out of line" in games where they can give themselves an excuse to play or overplay certain hands without looking completely foolish. It is in these games where you have the best opportunity to take them off. The following is a list from worst to best, of the games you want to play against someone on tilt.

**Jacks of better draw poker** — Good players almost can't steam in this game without obviously taking the worst of it. They

47

can't open with less than jacks and they know they are crazy to call an opener with less than kings.

**Razz** — This is another game that keeps almost all good players from steaming. If you don't have a good starting hand, it is hard to find an excuse to play.

**Seven-card stud** — Steaming in this game is far more dangerous at the $15-$30 level or lower where the ante is proportionally smaller. However, the larger games have such a large ante that the steamer is not taking that much the worst of it if he has the worst of it at all.

**Omaha (high only)** — A player who is steaming can find an excuse to play almost every hand before the flop. Unfortunately, a good player doesn't hurt himself that badly by playing this way as long as he plays well after the flop.

**Lowball draw** — A desperate player can get into a lot of trouble in this game. It all depends on how much he loosens up. Playing two card draws in late position won't hurt him too much. If he gets further out of line, he's dead.

**Seven-card stud hi-lo split eight-or-better** — This is another game where you can find an excuse to play a lot of hands if you want to. As in seven-card stud high, the penalty for this practice is greater for those games where the ante is proportionally smaller.

**Hold 'em** — This is, in my opinion, the third best game to play against steamers. Since any two cards can win, the desperate player is apt to see a lot of flops. He will usually regret it.

**California Draw** — This game is open blind, high draw. Unlike jacks or better you can open with anything and a steaming player is apt to do just that. In a seven or eight handed game this will usually be suicide for him and great for you.

**Omaha hi-lo split 8-or-better** — As in regular Omaha, a player on tilt will find excuses to play a lot of hands. However, unlike regular Omaha, playing a bad hand is apt to get him into even further trouble on the later betting rounds. You can, therefore, just sit back and wait for him to hang himself.

# Never Go Broke

If you are trying to play poker for a living, you should never risk going broke.

No matter how great a game might be, it isn't worth playing in if a big loss will put you out of action. This is not just common sense, it can also be proven mathematically. If you are, in fact, a winning player, it can be shown that you will make more money in the long run if you don't play in games so large that you are in jeopardy of having to stop playing altogether or even having to reduce your stakes for a while.

In other words, if you have a $2,000 bankroll and are currently playing $5-$10, you should not jump into a juicy $20-$40 game. Even if you don't go broke, you risk losing so much that you can no longer comfortably play $5-$10 but must grind your way back up at lower stakes.

If the $20-$40 is really that great, your best option would be to sell a large "piece" of yourself and then go play in the game that has now become reasonable stakes for you. If you can't find someone to buy a piece, you must pass the game.

Suppose, however, you found a great $10-$20 game with this same $2,000 bankroll. If you can't find a partner, should you still pass?

Maybe not. If this game figures to earn you three or four times as much per hour as your typical $5-$10 game, you should consider playing — even on a short bankroll. However, you should not play your best game!

By this, I mean you shouldn't play the optimum strategy, but instead should play a strategy where maintaining your bankroll is a major consideration. This may cut your earning potential in half, but you will still be earning one and a half to two times as much as normal.

The question is, how should one play when one is worried about the bankroll? The obvious answer is to play very tight. However, there is more to it than that.

The more accurate answer is to play in such a way as to win as large a percent of the pots you play as possible. Winning extra bets takes a back seat to making sure you win the pot. This means for one thing never to "slow play" anything other than cinch hands.

If, for instance, you have three rolled up deuces in seven-card stud and an ace raises on your right, you should reraise. Get the pot head up rather than suck in players behind you who might out draw you. This play figures to cost you some profits, but with a short bankroll it is the right move, as it will greatly increase your chances of winning the pot.

To make sure you understand the principle, I will change the example slightly. You have three deuces again and an ace raises again. But this time a bunch of other players have already called the raiser. I would not reraise on a short bankroll.

I am not slow playing, but am rather trying to keep the pot fairly small. This way, the other players don't get "tied on" to their hands due to the huge pots offered them. Once again, this play cuts into your profits, but it increases your chances of winning the pot.

Playing extra tight, especially in the early betting rounds, is also important on a short bankroll. You should consider throwing away hands such as ace-queen in hold 'em or a four-card rough seven in lowball. Never call an open pair in seven-card stud with one high pair unless you are sure he doesn't have trips. Throw away most three flushes that break off on fourth street.

The general principal here is that if there is a good chance you will lose a lot of money on a hand, you're better off not getting involved at all. Marginally profitable calls shouldn't be made.

As a final note, let me mention that these foregoing principles also apply to a situation besides playing in a game you can't really afford. They also apply to tournament play, especially when you find yourself at an easy table. Once again, the main consideration is not going broke. (I discuss tournaments at much greater length in *Sklansky on Poker*.)

# Four Case Studies

To be a successful poker player you ought not to lie to yourself. Here are four people who did.

**Case No. 1.** This player has to believe in his heart that he is the very best. I don't think he could handle it otherwise. To avoid facing the truth he plays in a manner that is frequently outlandish, ostensibly to make money in the long run. But he plays this way far too often and the long run never arrives. The real reason he plays this way is so he can keep on telling himself he is the best and that the reason for his temporary lack of success is his "advertising." Once he buckles down to solid play his true greatness will show. But in my opinion, he can never buckle down for fear that it won't. If he could only admit this, he'd would be a lot better off.

**Case No. 2.** Similar to case No. 1, this female player had to make others and herself believe she can play as well as any man. But she can't. So to keep herself and others from knowing the truth she steams when she is losing. And sometimes gets high. This is embarrassing, of course, but not as embarrassing as not being successful in the bigger games even while playing her best. So she gave herself an excuse. Of course, she went broke. Now she deals. She claims that she'd rather have the steady income and lack of pressure even though she knows she could make a lot more by playing, if she had to. She really believes it. Do you?

**Case No. 3.** On the opposite side of the coin we have a man who never steams, never takes chances, never plays above three and six limit, and has no money. Of course, if he did have money, he would show those $10-$20 and $15-$30 players that he is just as good or better than they are. It's just that it's hard to build up a bankroll in the smaller games. It would seem that the solution would be to get staked in the bigger games. This is common among good players.

He says he won't do this because he doesn't want the responsibility. I say the real reason is that, like Cases No.1 and 2, he is afraid to find out the truth. This way he can still lie to himself.

**Case No. 4.** This player insists on maintaining that you can predict or change luck, and that cards do not necessarily approximately break even in the long run. Of course, if you believe this, it is not necessary that you learn to play that well. Secondly, if you believe this, you don't have to be ashamed that you don't do as well as other players. You are just not as lucky. Thus once again we have a player who has convinced himself of something that isn't true because the real truth is simply too painful to face.

While I did have four specific people in mind when I wrote this piece, the fact is that there are many players who fit one of these molds. In one way or another they find excuses rather than admit that they don't play as well as they think they do. The shame of it is that many of these people could become quite successful poker players if they would only swallow their pride and do some studying. This is, of course, also hard for them since they don't want to admit that after all their years of experience they could still learn a lot from a book. If they could do this and admit to themselves that there will still be others better than them, then a lot of these players could be doing quite a bit better than they are doing now. Financially and otherwise.

# Ranking The Players

The main problem with ranking the best players arises because there are different types of poker situations and different players are best in each type. These categories are:

1. Tournaments (freezeout types)
2. Shorthanded games
3. Ring games
4. Tough games
5. Easier games
6. Efficiency at your best
7. Efficiency when losing

There is no poker player alive who is in the top five in all categories for a particular game. This is because different skills are required to master each category.

For instance, shorthanded poker games are significantly different than "ring games," and require significantly different skills. There are many excellent shorthanded players who lose much of their advantage when the game fills up. Shorthanded and heads-up games are instinctual, while ring games are more technical. On the other hand there are players who would achieve a higher ranking for their play in full games though they may also do well in shorthanded games.

It may be surprising to you that tougher games and easier games should be separated into two different categories. After all, it would seem that those players who fared best in tough games would do the best in easier games as well. However, this isn't the case.

It frequently occurs that champion players who fare well against other experts don't win as much in easier games as specialists in these games do. For instance, there are players who have consistently beaten the best at the highest limits, who I don't think would do as well in a game such as $30-$60 as some of the middle limit experts do. This is true even though these middle limit experts would have difficulty against the superstars. This is because it takes different talents to play weaker players.

What about the bottom line? Should the title of best player be accorded to the ones who "get the money?" By this criteria we would have a much different list than if we just evaluated players when they are playing their best. The fact of the matter is that some of these "brilliant" players do not win as much money at the end of the year as their less brilliant counterparts. This is because they don't choose their games well and they "go on tilt." If you start playing badly just because you are losing, in a desperate attempt to get even for the day, it isn't clear you deserve to be called the best player.

Finally, we come to tournament play. Once again, we have a situation where the best strategy is quite a bit different from what would be best in regular games. Thus, we once again get a different list of best players. Specifically, players who don't have the patience to play their best in normal games, find that the "captive audience" nature of a tournament forces them to play well.

Aggressive players find that their styles are especially suited to tournaments, since other players are reluctant to expend the chips necessary to keep them honest. Tournaments are also okay for the superstars who are used to playing against players playing their best, as most players in a tournament tend to do. However, ironically, it is those players who are very successful at grinding out excellent money against weaker players who have the most difficulty during freezeout tournaments.

# Saving Various
# Forms of Poker

If you play poker in the legal cardrooms of California, Nevada, or elsewhere you must have noticed that some games are quite a bit more popular than others. In California, lowball is far more widespread than jacks or better, and "California" draw is virtually nonexistent. In Nevada, limit hold 'em, especially for higher stakes, is quite a bit rarer than seven stud.[4]

No-limit hold 'em is never played except during tournaments. Razz and hi-lo split are hard to find. On the other hand, the relatively new game of Omaha is now played quite a bit.

The foregoing is especially bad for you if your best game is one of those becoming extinct. Is there a way to save these endangered games? I have some ideas and I will mention them shortly. First, however, it is important to understand what is causing this syndrome.

Why do people play poker? If you are a professional player, the answer would simply be to make money. That, however, is not the reason most people play. Whether they admit it or not, their reason is to have fun.

Now, it is true that the mere challenge of making money in a poker game is fun in itself, especially for a serious amateur. However, for most amateurs the fact that they have a good chance to win only by playing in a way that is not fun turns them off to those games where this is true.

No matter what poker game you play, you have the choice of whether to play to win or play to have fun. You can't do both. However, in some games it is easier to have fun and still win than in other games. Not surprisingly, it is those games that are far more

---

[4]This essay was originally written before the legalization of stud and hold 'em in California.

popular. Thus, we have the ironic result that the games the skillful player beats most often, are usually much tougher and not as widespread as those games where the weak player has a better chance to win (at least over the short run).

So what is the remedy? The answer is to change the structure of some games so that players who are there to have fun will have a 30 to 40 percent chance of winning for an individual session. This should keep them coming back. Doing this should help the professional player also. He might not have as high a percentage of winning days, but his long run profits would certainly increase since his competition would be weaker. Everyone would be happier.

The basic principle behind my suggestion stems from the fact that it is not fun to fold hands, especially not at the beginning, thus putting yourself immediately out of action and being forced to do nothing for the next few minutes. However, in some types of games you can get out of line on that first betting round and still have a decent chance to win. This is true of the popular games of seven-card stud, lowball, and Omaha, but not of the others. The solution is to change these other games in such a way that those players who play a lot of starting hands are not so horribly punished.

I have three suggestions.

1. In games such as hold 'em and California draw where there is no ante and large blinds, I would add an ante and decrease the blinds.

2. In games such as hold 'em and hi-lo split I would allow no raise (or maybe one raise only) on the first betting round.

3. I would consider adding a wrinkle where the player is originally dealt more cards than he starts with but has to discard one. This makes it more likely that he will start with a decent hand. It is especially effective in razz and hi-lo split.

I hope you see why all these ideas make it easier for a loose player to win.

Interestingly enough, none of these innovations is really original. They are in fact quite common in home games. And wouldn't you rather have these home game players playing with you?

# Why I Don't
# Like Seven-Card Stud

Remember the first time you ate a grapefruit? Probably not, but I do, and I also remember almost everything else just like it was yesterday. Undoubtedly this has helped me in my poker career, as I can replay all of the relevant hands I have played and constantly reevaluate to see if I could have used a better strategy.

Unfortunately, having this kind of long term memory has little to do with the short term ability to memorize (and then quickly forget) cards that you have seen. This keeps me from being a great gin player, hurts me in my blackjack play, and is a big disadvantage when playing seven-card stud.

I freely admit that my worst game is stud.[5] My not being able to memorize all the cards that are exposed and then folded is the main reason. The fact of the matter is that the proper strategy can change dramatically based on the cards that are out. This is true for three reasons.

1. Your chances of improving or making your hands can change quite a lot based on which cards you have seen;
2. The same is true of your opponent's hands, but most importantly...
3. What you read your opponent for can easily change based on the cards you have seen.

It is the third category that the seven-card stud superstars shine. It works two ways. For one thing, great players will adjust their assessment of another player's hand, since they know that he is also looking at the exposed cards. Thus, if their opponent plays a seven up on third street with one other seven showing, they will almost

---

[5]This was written a long time ago and is no longer true.

completely eliminate a pair of sevens for their assessment of his hand, since they know that a decent player will rarely play a medium pair when one of them is already gone.

A more advanced way to use the cards that are out to change your assessment of an opponent's hand has to do with adjusting probabilities when cards are exposed. For instance, suppose a player raises with an ace showing on third street and you know that he would make this play with a pair of aces, or a buried pair, or a three card flush. Normally, his raise would mean that he was better than 50 percent to have specifically two aces rather than either of the other two hands. However, this would not be so if there was one other ace showing. Thus, a pair of queens, for instance, would be clearly playable against it (especially when you add in the fact that even if he started with aces, it is about half as likely as normal that he would make three aces).

The foregoing is just the tip of the iceberg as far as how expert stud players alter their strategy based on the cards that are shown. These strategy changes are much more important than most players realize and thus put otherwise good players who have difficulty memorizing cards at a big disadvantage.

However, this is not the only reason why I don't like seven-card stud. There are a few problems with the game as far as most pros are concerned. For one, there are too many automatic "chasing" situations where you must call with the obvious second best hand with more cards to come, simply because of the pot odds compared to your chances of improvement. *You must thus play the same way a bad player would.* It does you little good on fifth and sixth street to know you are beat. Betting strategy is also too automatic, as the high board is usually betting whether it be an expert or a sucker. There are less opportunities for a check raise than in a game like hold 'em. Another way stud differs from hold 'em is that in stud the last card is down. A great card reader in hold 'em will almost always know when his opponent has made his hand and can therefore act accordingly, but this is not so in stud.

To put it another way, suppose you were playing with marked cards, a situation that pros figuratively find themselves in against weak amateurs. Would you rather be playing seven-card stud or hold 'em with these marked cards?

So you see now, I think, why I like hold 'em better than seven-card stud, and I have not even given all the reasons (such as that the best hand holds up more often in hold 'em). I don't play stud as well, but my ideas are not just sour grapefruits.

# A Tidbit to Think About

Did you ever notice that when all the cards are out and someone bets in a heads-up pot the other player frequently agonizes about calling? Yet that same player rarely has to think about whether or not to bet when it is checked to him. But this should not be, because whether to bet often is a tougher decision than whether to call. If there is $120 in the pot and your opponent bets $20, you normally should call if you assess your winning chances to be anywhere from about 15 percent to 60 percent. This is a wide range. Calls frequently should be automatic. Betting, however, is a much tougher decision. Not only might you consider the chances of running a successful bluff, you also must pinpoint your chances of success before deciding to value bet a good but not great hand. And to evaluate a value bet, you must not only assess the chances that you have the best hand, but also the chances that you will get called by a worse hand. This means that you will sometimes bet with a hand that has a 55 percent chance to be the best, and sometimes check with one that has a 70 percent chance. So, think more about your bets and less about your calls on that last round of betting.

# Drawing to the Second Best Hand

The ability to fold correctly when you suspect you are drawing dead or with too little chance of ending up with the best hand is one attribute that distinguishes a good player from an average one.

Equally important in determining whether a hand that needs improvement is worth a call is the question of whether the hand will win even if you do make it. Your hand might lose in a variety of ways because you are drawing dead — that is, the hand you are looking to make is already beaten by your opponent. For example, when that open pair bets into your four flush or a possible straight, he might be betting a full house. It can also happen that you make your hand but your opponent makes an even better hand (even though you weren't drawing dead.) Your four flush might, for example, be up against three-of-a-kind. You may make your flush, but your opponent may very well make a full house.

In such situations you must reduce your odds of winning and sometimes throw your hand away. For instance, a four flush against three-of-a-kind in seven-card stud is a much greater underdog than a four flush against two pair because trips is more than twice as likely to improve to a full house.

To repeat, the ability to fold correctly when you suspect you are drawing dead or with too little chance of ending up with the best hand is one attribute that distinguishes a good player from an average one. On the other hand, poor players are likely to call thoughtlessly "on the come." They do not consider that they may be drawing dead; and when they're not drawing dead, they do not adjust their chances of ending up with the best hand, taking into account the possibility of an opponent's making a bigger hand than their own.

In hold 'em and other community-card games, you can sometimes draw dead because the cards that will give you the hand you want will also give your opponent an even better hand. Suppose in hold 'em you are holding

your opponent is holding

and the board is

If a queen falls on the end, you make a straight and a straight beats three jacks. However, the queen also happens to give your opponent a full house. Similarly, if you hold

and the board is

there is no card in the deck that will make you a winner against an opponent holding the A♥ and another heart. A heart at the end gives you a king-high flush, but it gives your opponent an ace-high flush.

When you think your opponent might beat you even if you make your hand, you must adjust your odds of winning before comparing them to the pot odds you are getting. Let's say you are a 5-to-1 underdog to make your hand, and you are getting 7-to-1 from the pot. On the surface your hand is worth a call. But suppose you feel there is a 30 percent chance your opponent will make a hand that beats the one your are trying to make. Should you still call? As a 5-to-1 underdog you are going to make your hand one-sixth of the time, which is 16⅔ percent. However, of that 16⅔ percent, your hand will be good only 70 percent of the time. All of a sudden, instead of winning 16⅔ percent of the time, you will win only about 11⅔ percent of the time.

$$11\tfrac{2}{3} = (16\tfrac{2}{3})(.70)$$

You go from a 5-to-1 shot to approximately a 7½-to-1 shot.

$$7.57 = \left( \frac{100 - 11\tfrac{2}{3}}{11\tfrac{2}{3}} \right)$$

What appeared to be an easy call has become a fold.

In general, you don't need to calculate your chances of winning so precisely. When there is a chance of drawing dead or being out drawn after you make your hand, you had better throw away most of your close plays because they will swing into losing plays. You have to overcome the double adversity of having the worst hand in the first place and the possibility of not winning when you make the hand you are hoping to make. To call a bet in such a situation requires very good pot odds indeed.

# A Note on Extra Outs

Just as many players overlook the effects of position and exposed cards and the possibility of drawing dead to lower the value of a hand, so too do they sometimes overlook *extra outs to* increase the value of a hand.

An out is a way of improving your hand. With four hearts your only out is another heart. But suppose you have two pair along with the four flush and are against what looks like aces up. Now you have two outs — making a flush and a full house.

Suppose you have a four flush, two pair and an inside straight draw. Now you have three outs — that is, three ways of beating your opponent who has the aces-up, assuming that player doesn't fill.

Each extra out increases the value of your hand, and it increases it considerably more than may at first be apparent. Starting off with a two flush and a pair in seven-card stud is significantly better than starting with a pair and no two flush. In hold 'em a back-door straight (that is, a possible straight requiring two perfect cards at the end) or a backdoor flush draw along with a pair may be enough to change a fold to a call.

To see how much effect these extra outs have, let's say we assess our hand as a 7-to-1 underdog. Now we notice we have an extra out that is about 20-to-1 against coming in. By itself, that extra out is a long shot, but it adds tremendously to our chances of improving. Changing those 7-to-1 and 20-to-1 odds to percentages we have a 12½ percent chance and about a 5 percent chance, which, added together, comes to approximately 17½ percent. Returning from percentages to odds, we see that the extra out has dropped us from a 7-to-1 underdog to approximately a 4¾-to-1 underdog.[6]

$$4.714 \ = \ \frac{100 - 17.5}{17.5}$$

With pot odds of, say 5-to-1 or 6-to-1, a hand we would have folded now becomes one worth playing. Always be aware of extra outs. Otherwise, you may fold hands with which you should have called.

---

[6]This calculation assumes the two events are mutually exclusive.

# Risking a Reraise

Keep in mind that when you bet after someone else has checked, you are not just risking the money that you bet. You also are reopening his opportunity to cost you more money by raising. The same point holds true when you raise someone who has bet. You risk not only the cost of your raise, but also a reraise. This concept is especially important when you are playing no-limit poker and have a mediocre hand that has a small chance of turning into a "monster." If your bet or raise has elicited a reraise that forces you to fold a hand with winning chances, you probably made a bad play. (Notice that this idea does not apply when you are first to act and, thus, can't keep your opponent from betting more anyway. It also, of course, doesn't apply when either you or he is all-in.)

# Standing Pat

In my book, *The Theory of Poker*, I mention a play I sometimes make in jacks or better draw poker where I stand pat with just one pair of aces. I do this not to bluff, but rather to stop a bluff. If you are against only one opponent who is obviously on the come for a straight or flush (because he didn't open but then backed in in late position and drew one card) standing pat with two aces is frequently the best play. This is because your standing pat will keep most players from even considering a bluff when they miss their hand, whereas if you draw cards they will occasionally bluff. If you don't draw any cards, you simply fold when your opponent bets, knowing that he must have you beaten. However, if you draw cards and he bets, you might throw away the winning hand. If you decide to call when he bets, you figure to lose money after the draw since most players will bluff less frequently than they will make their hand. Either way, your drawing cards hurts you (unless you have a "tell" on the guy and will thus call him only when he's bluffing).

There are some reasons to draw cards (usually three) with your two aces. Obviously, if your opponent is just as likely to bluff even when you stand pat, then you might as well draw. However, only expert players would attempt to bluff out a pat hand. But it is also better to draw if this will make your opponent bluff with such a high frequency that more of his bets will be on "busts" than on legitimate hands. Against such wild players you will make money after the draw if you take three cards and call when he bets.

In general, however, your opponent will not usually be a wild bluffer or capable of trying to bluff out a pat hand. Still, there is one other reason to draw, namely, the possibility that you will make a full house when he makes his straight or flush. When this happens your drawing cards not only saves you the pot, but figures to make you two after the draw bets as well. This factor, however, is negligible when compared to what you gain by stopping his bluffs.

To prove this I will now show how the play can be right even with three-of-a-kind.

Let's say you open as the dealer with three kings. A player backs in in very late position. His most likely hands are a flush draw (a 21 percent shot to hit), a twelve-way straight draw (25 percent) or a sixteen-way straight draw (33 percent). Occasionally, he will have even better chances with a straight flush draw. If you are playing in a full $25-$50 game there would now be $90 in the pot. Let's say on average he has a 30 percent chance to hit his hand. Now assume he will never bluff if you stand pat but will bluff with 10 percent of his hands if you draw. Let us now calculate your mathematical expectation when drawing and standing pat.

The calculation for standing pat is easy. It is simply 70 percent of $90 or $63.

$$\$63 = (.7)(\$90)$$

Drawing is more complicated. Since you will improve 11 percent of the time, we have the following possible results. (I assume in these calculations that you will always fold when you don't improve if he bets, since he is a 30-10 favorite to have it and you are only getting 140-50 odds. I also assume that you will make $100 after the draw or $190 total if you both improve.)

### Calculation for Drawing 2 Cards

| Play of Hand | Probability | Result |
|---|---|---|
| You miss, he bets, you fold | $(.89)(.40) = .376$ | 0 |
| You miss, he gives up | $(.89)(.60) = .534$ | +90 |
| You improve, he gives up | $(.11)(.60) = .066$ | +90 |
| You improve, he improves | $(.11)(.30) = .033$ | +190 |
| You improve, he bluffs | $(.11)(.10) = .011$ | +140 |

Your total expectation is thus $61.81.

$$\$61.81 \ = \ (.376)(\$0) + (.534)(\$90) + (.066)(\$90) +$$
$$(.033)(\$190) + (.011)(\$140)$$

You average $1.19 a hand better against a player who plays in this manner when you stand pat on three kings!

$$\$1.19 \ = \ \$63.00 - \$61.81$$

I leave it up to the reader to deduce the full impact of this result to poker strategy in general.[7]

---

[7]This is how I ended this essay years ago. I'll make it easier on you now. What this example illustrates is how much you gain when you know your opponent will never bluff. So if it costs you some money to manipulate him into playing that way against you it is money well spent.

# Jackpot Game
# Strategy Changes

It has been suggested that you should not change your play in a jackpot lowball game regardless of the size of the jackpot.[8] This is wrong. While it is true that most players change their play much more than they should to try to hit the jackpot, there are times when it is clearly worth changing strategies, especially when the jackpot is large. I will give two examples:

You have a pat

You are playing $5-$10 blind with a $5,000 jackpot. (Lowball jackpots are paid when you get a 6-4 low beaten.) Your opponent has raised you twice and now draws a card. He is probably drawing to a bicycle. If you discard your eight, you have about a one percent chance of hitting the jackpot, which is far more important than the fact that your chances of winning the pot decrease by about 17%.

In high draw (where the jackpot is awarded when aces full or better is beaten) the most obvious time to change your play occurs when you have aces-up before the draw and you are sure you are up against trips. The correct play here is normally to break your aces up and draw three but you shouldn't with any kind of decent jackpot.

---

[8]Jackpot games are presently illegal at non-Indian casinos in California, but they can be found elsewhere.

In general when the lowball jackpot is large, you should never keep a nine in your hand and rarely keep an eight if throwing them away will result in a six-four draw. In high (draw) poker you should play aces-up in some marginal situations and never keep a kicker to three-of-a-kind. The small errors involved here are minor when compared to your increased chances of hitting the jackpot.

# Catching Bluffers

One of the most important skills needed to be a winning poker player is the ability to assess the probability that an opponent's bet is a bluff. This is especially so on the last round of betting. When someone does bet into you on the last round you are usually in trouble, unless your hand is good enough to raise with. If it is not worth a raise, you are generally holding a hand that probably can't beat him if he really has what he is representing. Usually, your only hope in such a situation is that he's bluffing.

When you have a mediocre hand that can only beat a bluff, you should not necessarily fold just because you think your opponent is probably not bluffing. The reason for this stems from the odds you are getting from the pot. If for instance you think there is a 75 percent chance that your opponent has the hand he is representing and a 25 percent chance he is bluffing, you still must call if the pot is offering you better than 3-to-1 odds.

So how does one evaluate the chances that a player is bluffing? A lot of it has to do with experience and knowing your players. I won't go into that here. I would like to address one particular aspect of this problem. That is the propensity of many players to confuse frequent *bluffers* with frequent *bettors*. They are not necessarily the same thing.

To be more precise, what I am saying is that a tight player who rarely bets marginal hands for value but does sometimes bluff may find a higher proportion of his bets are bluffs than the aggressive player who bets many more legitimate hands and bluffs as well.

There is a natural tendency to call the aggressive player and to fold against the tight player when each bets on the end, but both strategies may be wrong. If the aggressive player will bet just as many "bust-outs" as the tight player, his ratio of bluffs to legitimate hands is actually lower than the ratio for the tight player. Thus, with a mediocre hand that is only good as a "bluff catcher," you would be more apt to call the tight player than the aggressive one. On the other side of the coin it is important to understand these concepts when you yourself are the bettor. Specifically, if your image is that of a tight player who rarely bluffs, your counter strategy should of course be to try a bluff that might not work for someone else. However, you shouldn't bet only fair hands, as you will only be called if you are beaten. Conversely, if you are perceived as a frequent bluffer, you should rarely bluff but should bet your fair hands for value since you will be called by worse hands.

# Call or Raise?

Beginning poker players assume that the better your hand is, the better it is to raise with it. Experienced players know that this is not always true. They know that there are many situations where it is right to raise with a good hand but not with a great hand. Even experienced players, however, may not be aware that there are quite a few different types of situations where you should raise with a good hand, call with a better hand, but raise with a still better hand. Here are some examples:

**Lowball draw** — You open the pot for a raise. A loose player calls behind you. The blind reraises. Your correct play is probably to call with pat rough eights, raise with good eights or rough sevens, call with good sevens, and raise with a seven-four or better. Without going into detail I can tell you that the basic reason for this is that you don't want to knock out a third party who is probably drawing dead unless you would welcome a reraise.

**Hold 'em** — Eight players have called before the flop and you are in the blind. You should raise with two nines or two aces in the pocket but probably not with two jacks or two queens. This seems very strange but it can be demonstrated mathematically as well as logically. Basically, you raise with aces because of the strength of your hand and with nines because you are getting 8-to-1 odds on your raise and you might flop a set. Of course, jacks and queens could flop a set also but they can win frequently without it. The problem is that it is much harder for these pairs to win by themselves if you give your hand away and double the pot size, especially in early position.

**Draw poker, jacks or better to open** — A tight player opens and a good player raises. You are next. Call with medium trips. Raise with big trips. Call with three aces or a straight. Raise with a flush or better. This is similar to the lowball example already given. Though you fear the raiser, you must knock out the opener when you have big trips to keep him from drawing to aces. (With medium trips, reraising is too dangerous, since you are too likely to have a worse hand than the raiser. Still, you call because of pot odds.) You can, however, afford to keep the opener in when you have three aces or a straight. With a flush or better you're not too worried about the raise and can stand a reraise so you should usually make it three bets yourself.

**Lowball draw** — You open and a very tight player in the blind raises. He must draw first and everyone else is out. A good strategy against him would be to reraise with your pat nines, sevens, and bicycles; and to just call with your eights and rough sixes. You raise with your nines to get him to "break" his hand or as a prelude to a bluff. You call with your eights to "hold him dead" if he has a nine. You reraise with your sevens, since you are less worried about his breaking a nine and are likely to have the best hand. Sixes (especially rough ones) you can call with against a very tight player in order to try to get two or three double bets after the draw, though the play is debatable when the sevens rule is in effect. A bicycle or smooth six should not be slowplayed, however, since you shouldn't eliminate the possibility of winning seven or eight bets before the draw. (I admit this example is not as clear cut as the first three. I give it simply to show how there can be logical reasons for even two "breaks" in discontinuous raising strategy.)

# Mercy of Luck

Few people realize how much even expert players are at the mercy of luck in the short run. One of the most dramatic ways to show this is by the following two statements.

1. No one could beat a draw game if they were never dealt a pat straight or better.
2. No one could beat a lowball game if they were never dealt a pat seven-four or better.

Without these occasional super hands being dealt to them even expert players could at best hope to break even. A $25-$50 draw expert who averages $40 an hour figures to get a pat hand about once every three hours and each one of those hands averages about $120 profit. His hourly win thus comes from his pat hands. Similarly a $30-$60 lowball expert who averages $50 per hour figures to be dealt a pat "monster" about once every five hours and they should win him an average of about $250 per time.

# An Expert Lowball Play

It is not often that the play of a lowball draw hand requires the use of several advanced poker concepts, but one did come up a while back in a $50-$100 game at the Bicycle Club.

The structure of the game requires a $25 blind on the button and a $25 and $50 blind in the first two seats to the left of the button.

In this particular hand, I was dealt a pat

one seat to the right of the button. The first four players folded and I, of course, opened for $100 dollars. A very tough player called $75 more on the button. The small blind folded but the big blind raised to $150. I did not reraise but simply called the $150. The tough player also called.

The big blind drew one card, I stood pat and the tough player drew one. After the draw the big blind checked, I bet and the tough player raised! I called and beat his straight seven. ·

Experienced lowball players should see that I played this hand quite strangely and on the surface, incorrectly. The standard play would be to raise to $200 before the draw. Furthermore, it is usually correct to throw rough sevens away when you are raised after the draw, but in this case I didn't even consider folding.

Because I understand how to intertwine various poker concepts, I was able to see that this was a unique situation where the standard play was not the best. However, it could only occur with a specific type of hand against a specific type of player. I would have reraised before the draw with my hand if it had been a little better or a little worse. Even with my 7♠6♦4♥3♣2♠, I would have reraised if my opponent had been a little tighter or a little looser. Only under precise conditions could my play be right. Let's see why.

The first thing to understand is that I don't need that strong a hand to open one seat to the right of the button. Furthermore, I know that the tough player who came in behind me knows this. Thus, when I open, this player would probably raise with a pat hand or a strong one card draw. However, he would not call with a two card draw. Thus, when he flat calls I put him on a one card draw to a good eight or a rough seven. In other words, he is probably "drawing dead." When the blind raised I knew that the tough player would fold his hand if I reraised, and I didn't want to knock out a player who was probably dead. However, had this opponent been a more typical player who would likely call a second hundred after putting in that first hundred, a raise would have been clearly better on my part. The fact that he was one of those few players who would fold in the spot was one of the reasons I just called. Another factor that had to be taken into account was the unlikeliness that the tough player had a two card draw. Since most players could have a two card draw in this situation, a raise would once again be in order since they wouldn't be drawing dead. I'd be happy to see them stay in, but I'd want to charge them for the privilege.

Thus we can see, first of all, that my play can only be right if the opponent on the button is both drawing dead and will not call if there is a double bet back to him.

As to why I need specifically a good 7-6 to play this way, first notice that with a worse pat hand I can be less sure that I have the tough player drawing dead and would thus welcome the opportunity to knock him out. With a very good pat hand I would raise for a different reason, namely the opportunity to win a bunch of bets from the original raiser in the big blind. With a 7-6 low I can't be that sure I have the best hand. Also, by just calling I keep him from breaking certain pat hands and thus "hold him dead."

Finally the advanced concept that applied to the after the draw play is of the psychological variety. It is that when you show weakness your opponent is more likely to bluff or bet or raise for value with less than normal hands. This is exactly what happened in this case. My weak play before the draw persuaded my expert opponent to raise with a weaker than normal hand. Understanding this, my call became automatic. All in all my "abnormal" strategy almost certainly gained me an extra $200.

# Checking a Seven

In my book *Sklansky on Poker* I give some advice on when it is right to check a seven in lowball draw. In this essay I'd like to expand on those times when it is correct to check a seven. Of course the situation occurs so infrequently that knowing about it will not make you (or save you) very much money. However, understanding the logic will be quite helpful in that it can lead you to the proper way to think about poker situations in general.

For those of you who are not familiar with the "sevens rule," used in California cardrooms, it states that if you check a seven low or better and then call, you must refund the after-the-draw-bet(s) if you have the best hand. This rule means that you are almost always better off betting your sevens than checking and calling.

Now, it is possible that you will be in a situation where you will check and then fold if someone bets. If you are quite sure that your seven low is no good, the existence of the sevens rule has no bearing on your play. Rather, it is only the play of checking and then calling with a seven that needs analysis.

The fact is that if you plan to call with your seven, if you check, it is almost always better to bet the hand yourself. That way if you do have the best hand you will not have to refund the after-the-draw-bet.

One time to check a seven occurs in a multi-way pot where you are already worried that you don't have the best hand. You check with the intention of folding if there is a bet and a raise behind you, or maybe even if there is a bet and call behind you. Your plans are to make a "crying call" only if one player bets and everyone else folds.

In a heads-up pot it is even less likely that it is correct to check and then call with a seven. However, previously I did write about a hypothetical example of where it would be the right play. I then went on to prove it mathematically. This time I will explain it in more general terms.

In general, in order for it to be correct to check and call with a seven low in a heads-up situation, two criteria must be met:

1. Your opponent must be capable of occasionally raising you without the best hand, and
2. Your hand must be very obvious, almost as if it were face up.

Obviously you would be forced to check your seven or even six low if you had inadvertently turned your cards up. You would then have to call a bet, since your opponent now has a free shot to bluff you out at no further risk to himself (he gets his money back if you call). In practice this situation usually occurs when you have a rough pat seven and have not put in the last raise before the draw.

Even in this case however, you should usually bet your seven if you have only a fairly small chance of getting a call from a worse hand rather than a check and call. It is only when you also fear a raise from a possible worse hand that you may be in the rare situation where it is better to check and call.

If a raise from your opponent can't mean a worse hand than yours, you should simply bet and then fold if raised. On the other hand if your opponent will frequently raise with a worse hand than yours, the right play is to bet and then to call his raise. It is only in the situation where his raise highly probably means a better hand but occasionally means a worse hand (so that you are forced to usually lose two bets or risk getting bluffed out) that it may be right to check and call with your obvious rough pat sevens.

# Three Good Plays

I would like to tell you about three poker plays I have made in the past that I am quite proud of. They will also serve to show how seemingly "illogical" plays can in fact be correct. (I hasten to point out that the correct play can never really be illogical in the formal sense. It is only the everyday type of logic that people use that can be wrong. In fact I will use formal logic to justify the correctness of these three plays.)

The first play occurs in lowball draw and has happened to me more than once. A player opens the pot and I raise with a hand such as

He calls and draws one card. I throw the nine away. He now checks and I look down and see that I have caught a nine right back. I now bet. Many players don't understand this play. They reason that if a nine-four is good enough to bet, then why discard the nine? The answer is that each decision must be evaluated on its own merit. The nine should be discarded mainly because of the good chances to make a "monster" hand. However, the nine I caught still calls for a value bet especially because I drew a card.

The second play occurred in a limit hold 'em game. I held the

There was no bet on the flop. After the fourth card the board showed

of different suits. An aggressive player bet and I called. The last card was another deuce. We both checked and I won the pot with ace high. But it wasn't my fourth street call that was the expert play. It was my readiness to fold on fifth street that was. When the hand was over, my opponent said "It's a good thing I didn't bet on the end, since you obviously were going to call with ace high. I know you didn't just call hoping to catch an ace or four since you weren't getting good enough pot odds for that." But he was wrong. I would have folded if he'd bet again. I called on fourth street because of the possibility to improve my hand *plus* the possibility I would win a no-bet showdown on the end. However, I would have folded if he had bet on the end, unless I caught an ace or a four. It's just that I knew that even if I didn't catch an ace or a four, there was a reasonable chance the ace was the best hand *and* he would give up without "firing the last barrel." (By the way, this type of strategy of calling once in the hopes of a check on the next round is much more common among experts in no-limit poker.)

The third play I made was similar to the last one but it seems even stranger and more "illogical." However, to this day I consider it the best play I ever made in poker. It occurred many years ago in a $15-$30 hold 'em game in Reno. I raised with the

and got five calls. The flop came

The first player bet and I called, since I was getting high pot odds and had the possibility of catching an ace or king or a "backdoor" straight or flush. Two players called behind me. The next card was the

The first player bet again. I folded. This might seem crazy as I apparently caught about the best card I could catch. However, I knew my opponent. I was sure that the ace on the turn would scare the guy into checking unless he had at least aces and jacks. And that in fact was what he had.

# Two Special Plays

In this essay I will discuss two related types of plays that are quite advanced and should normally be used against very good players only. The first one I call the "just-in-case-bluff."

It is a well known concept in poker that you shouldn't necessarily bet your hand on the last betting round simply because you think you probably have your opponent beaten. Rather, in order to "bet for value" it is usually necessary that you expect to have the best hand, even after you are called. Thus many hands that you think beat your opponents' should, nevertheless, be checked when all the cards are out to avoid a bet that will lose more often than it will win.

However, situations do occur on the end in which you should bet decent hands even though you are quite sure you won't be called unless you are beaten. You should bet in this situation if you think your opponent will also fold a hand that is slightly better than yours.

The bet should be made even if you don't really expect him to have that hand. For example, it may be correct to bet a pat 10 low after the draw in lowball. If your opponent draws one card and checks after the draw (thus eliminating the possibility that he has a seven or better) most players automatically show down the pat 10. They reason that they won't get called by a jack or worse (since they stayed pat) and, in fact, will only get called if they are beaten. That is true, however they also don't figure to get called if their opponents have caught tens or maybe even nines.

This means that the size of the pot probably makes a just-in-case bluff worth doing. It will frequently be meaningless and will save you the pot only about 10 percent of the time. However, it will cost you a bet only about 20 percent of the time since the remaining 70 percent he will simply fold. So if the pot is more than twice the size of the bet, the play will show a long run profit.

An example of a just-in-case bluff in hold 'em would be when you have "top pair" with a mediocre kicker and a third card to a flush falls on the end. You may have the best hand still; you may have already had the second best hand; or that last card may have beaten you. That last card can help you as well as hurt you, as it now gives you the opportunity for a just-in-case bluff. That is because if you still bet after this card comes, a good player will frequently fold top pair with a higher kicker.

While the just-in-case bluff works better against tough opponents, my second play, the "two-way bet," absolutely requires that you be against an expert. The play also works better in a no-limit game.

Experts know that when they are faced with a very large bet on the last card, their normally good hands have turned into "bluff catchers." This means that their hands can only beat bluffs. They know that almost all players will only consider making a very big bet if they have super hands — or if they are bluffing. With lesser hands their opponents can be expected to check or bet a smaller amount.

Thus the expert doesn't really pay much attention to the strength of his own hand in these situations as long as it is somewhere between mediocre and very good, as they all figure to be of equal value when faced with a very large bet. Rather the expert simply tries to figure out whether his opponent is bluffing. If he thinks he is, he will call with his mediocre hand. If he doubts it, he will fold even with his very good hands.

The foregoing strategy can be countered with the two-way bet. The play is to make a big bet with your merely good hands even if you're not sure it is the best hand. Your bet can make you money in either of two ways. He may believe you have the nuts and fold a better hand than yours (thus turning your bet into a just-in-case bluff). He may also think your big bet is a typical bluff and call with a worse hand!

An example of the two-way bet could, for instance, occur in no-limit deuce-to-seven lowball when your opponent stands pat and you draw a card and make a rough nine low. Rather than make your normal moderate bet you should occasionally make a very large bet, not knowing whether you want a call or not. In no-limit hold 'em, an example of a time to consider a two-way bet would be when a flush card comes on the end, except this time you have quite a good hand yourself — trips or a straight. Your two way bet may make him suspicious enough to call you with a worse hand. Then again he may decide to fold a small flush.

# Playing Against the Redraw

There is a situation I would like to discuss that arises all of the time in seven-card stud and razz. On sixth street, player A obviously has the best hand and the best draw. Player B is drawing to beat player A's present hand, but even this will lose if player A also improves.

To give a specific example, let's say the players are playing seven-card lowball (razz). Player A has a

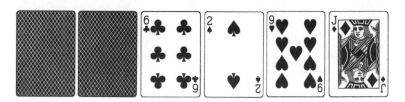

and Player B has

We can assume that player A (let's call him Matty from now on) has a nine low and is drawing to a six or seven low. Player B (call her Fedra) is clearly drawing to an eight low. How should they play their hands after the last card?

Most experienced players say that Matty should bet if he improves his hand and should check otherwise. If he does check, they say that Fedra should bet if she makes her eight low and maybe bluff occasionally if she does not. If she does bet, they recommend that Matty usually call with his 9 low for the size of the pot.

This analysis, however, is much too shallow, especially when tough players are involved. For one thing, if Matty follows this strategy, Fedra never has to call him when he bets, even if she makes her eight. Secondly, if he always checks when he misses, she never fears a check raise and can thus bet her eights with impunity. So you should now see that the normal recommended strategy for Matty is quite wrong.

A much better strategy is for Matty to check his hand most of the time, even when he makes his seven low. This play causes Julia to think twice about betting if she makes her eight low and virtually stops any thought of bluffing on her part. It is still marginally correct for her to bet if she makes her eight low but most of her profit from her play is gone since she will usually lose two bets when Matty makes his seven low. (Of course, Matty must occasionally check raise without improving so that she cannot automatically save a bet by throwing away her eight for a raise.)

The analogous play occurs in seven-card stud when an obvious pair of aces is against a lower pair going into the last card. If you usually try to check raise with aces up when you make that hand you frequently make an extra bet this way. If this play scares your opponent into checking two small pair behind you that's okay too since this will usually save you a bet when you don't improve.

# Betting Pat Hands in Lowball

What pat hands should you bet in lowball in last position after one or two opponents have checked to you? I assume a limit lowball game where the "sevens rule" (where you must bet a seven to win after the draw bets) is in effect. Your opponents' checking means that the best they could have is an eight low. Had you drawn a card, you would probably show a profit by betting all eights and nines. Since you stood pat, however, you must tighten up since you can't expect to get called unless they have a decent hand. Under most circumstances, you should show down all pat nines. On the other hand, you should certainly bet an eight-five or better since their check makes it very unlikely that they have a better hand. The tough decisions are the eight-sixes and the eight-sevens.

Against typical players the correct strategy may be surprising. It is this: If you think your opponent was drawing to an eight low, you must bet *less* pat eights for value than if you know he is drawing smoother.

Think about this for a minute. If a player draws one card to a seven-low and checks, the best he can have is an eight-seven. Even if he might be drawing to a six-low and checks, you can still bet a fairly rough eight since he may call you with a nine. The conclusion is that if a tight player draws one card and checks, you should probably bet a pat 8-7-4-x-x or better. However, against players who are drawing to good eight-lows, things change. If you know that he will check even if he makes his hand, but will call with an eight or even a nine, you cannot bet even a good eight-seven low for value. For example, suppose he was drawing to

He will call if he catches a nine, seven, six, four, or ace, and three of those five cards beat you. Thus, you need a hand like 8-6-4-x-x to bet your pat hand into this player.

The above analysis may seem like nit-picking, but experienced lowball players know how often they will be dealt specifically a pat eight-seven or rough eight-six. As to the question of how you know whether your opponent is drawing to an eight low, this is not always a judgement call. Weak tight players (who you know will not draw to eight-seven lows) sometimes will check in the dark to your pat hands. This marks them with smooth eight draws (because of the sevens rule) and you now know what to do against them.

# Check Raising in Hold 'em

Check-raising is an important tool for all kinds of poker, but nowhere is it as important as it is in hold 'em. The reason for this is that your position remains the same throughout all four rounds of betting. Thus, if you have to act first on the flop, you will also be first from then on.

This fact puts those players in early position in a hold 'em game at a tremendous disadvantage and forces them to play much tighter. However, a good deal of this disadvantage can be negated by liberal use of the check raise. In fact, the main thing that distinguishes the great hold 'em player from the good hold 'em player is knowing how to play in early positions, which means knowing when to check raise.

There are three main reasons to do a lot of check raising in hold 'em:

1. To get more money in the pot
2. To knock people out
3. To get free cards

Reason number three is just as important as the first two. If you are known as a frequent check raiser, other players will be more afraid to bet into you after you have checked. Since you will usually be checking with not so good hands, your previous check raises have allowed you to get a free card on these lesser hands. This free card may well win you the pot.

There is not enough space in this essay to even begin to go into the details of the correct check-raising strategy in hold 'em. However, I will give you one example.

When you have flopped a very good hand, especially a set of trips, in a head-up pot, you should usually check raise right on the flop, rather than wait for the double bet on fourth street. (We are

94

speaking of a limit game rather than no-limit.) For instance, if you have

in a $10-$20 game and the flop is

you should check, and if your opponent bets $10 you should make it $20. Most players in this situation just call on the flop, waiting to check raise on fourth street when the bet is $20, so they can make it $40.

The reason why this strategy is wrong is that it frequently will cost you $30, compared to my strategy, but it only gains $10 over my strategy, when it does work. This is because players will often check behind you on fourth street if you check. Even if they don't check, they will frequently fold when you make it $40, whereas if you had check raised on the flop and then bet all the way, they are more likely to call you all the way. This also is $30 better than if they bet on fourth street and then fold for a raise. Thus, we see that since waiting for fourth street to check raise can at most gain $10 over check-raising on the flop (in most cases), but can likely cost $30, you shouldn't do it unless you are almost sure it will work.

# Exposed Hand Problem

Most experts are quite adept at figuring out their opponents hands. This is, of course, one of the main reasons that they win.

However, strangely enough, it can occur that even when they know their opponent's hand they make the incorrect play! It is very true that I would rather be great at reading hands, than be great at figuring the right play if I saw the other player's cards. Still, the fact remains that most good readers are not taking optimum advantage of their ability.

Exposed hand problems work like this:

You can see your opponent's cards but he cannot see yours. Furthermore, he doesn't know that you can see his cards. Thus, the only difference between this situation, and you being able to read his cards, is that there is no doubt at all about what he has.

Here is a difficult problem.

The game is $10-$20 hold 'em. You know that your opponent has

The flop is

You have

giving you three sixes altogether.

He bets, you raise and he reraises. You just call which makes him think you may only have a flush draw. The next card is the

giving him three kings and you a full house. He bets again.

The question is, should you raise or just call? Remember there is still one card to come.

Of course, it is not good enough just to get the right answer. You must also have the right reason.

For this problem assume you are up against a typical player; i.e., if you raise on fourth street he will only call your raise and then check to you on the end if he does not improve. However, he will not throw his three kings away under any circumstances.

**Answer:** The correct answer is to raise. However, it is not simply because you have a full house. It is more complicated than that. It has to do with the two hearts on board. If there were not a two flush on the flop the answer would have been different. Let us look at this variation (no two flush) first.

If the board was instead:

and thus you can't have a flush draw, you do better in the long run if you only call his bet on fourth street and wait until the end to raise. If you do raise on fourth street, he will just call and then check and call on the end if he does not improve. You make two bets on fourth street and one bet on the end. If you just call on fourth street, however, he will come out betting on the end and you can raise him now. This also makes three bets: one on fourth street and two on fifth street. The difference is what happens when he catches a king, queen or deuce on the end to fill up and beat you. Now, not raising on fourth street has saved you a bet.

Situations arise like this all the time in poker. That is, situations where both of two alternative plays will win the same amount when they do win, but one of the alternatives loses less when it loses. The second alternative only loses one bet on fourth street while raising loses two.

I suspect that many readers thought the right answer to the original problem was to call. However, they overlooked the fact that there were two hearts on the flop, and that you know your opponent suspects you have a flush draw.

Why does this change things? Let's examine it.

If you just call on fourth street, you will save a bet (as opposed to raising) if a king, queen, or deuce falls. Thus, there are seven cards that can come off on the end that will make you glad you just called on fourth street. However, suppose a heart falls on the end (other than the queen or king of hearts).

These cards will scare him into checking and calling even if you didn't raise on fourth street. If you did raise, we assume he will still check and call on the end when the heart comes. There are 9 such scare cards. When one of these 9 cards comes on the end, your flat call on fourth street has cost you a bet.

In other words, there are 7 cards that can come on the end that make a call on fourth street 1 bet better for you, but 9 cards that make a call 1 bet worse. The other cards that can come make you 3 bets either way.

So assuming the opponent will play his hand as expected, it is better to raise.

# Last Round Strategies

It is very important to realize how the concepts pertaining to the last round of a poker hand can be radically different from the concepts you think about in earlier rounds. It is almost as if you are playing a different game. When I play, I frequently play the early and middle rounds rather quickly and smoothly only to stop before the last round to regroup my thoughts. I can't immediately switch my thoughts from early round strategies. I must pause and "remind" myself that it is the last round.

The reason why last round strategy can be so different from earlier rounds is that there are no more cards to come. This means that some of the possible reasons to bet on earlier rounds no longer apply. For one thing, you no longer have to bet to avoid giving your opponent a free card. He gets no more cards. Furthermore, *you* also get no more cards so that you cannot bet partially in the hopes of improving as you could earlier. Finally, you cannot bet (or check) in the hopes of setting something up for a future betting round, as this is the last round.

A classic example of the difference between last round and earlier round play is as follows:

You are playing seven-card stud and find yourself with *four jacks* on sixth street. Unfortunately, however, they are all showing. Your opponent shows

While a rational opponent will not call your sixth street bet with just three queens (which is what he must have had to call your fifth street bet), you still must bet to avoid giving him a free shot to catch

his fourth queen. However, if he does somehow call your bet, you have a much different situation on seventh street. Now you should certainly not bet. All you can do is lose more money as he will not call with a worse hand than yours. You are "betting into the wind."

As obvious as this situation is to expert players, beginners usually mess up even in simple situations like this. (In fact, every beginning player I ever asked as to what they would do on seventh street in this situation has said "bet.")

When the situation becomes more complicated, even great players frequently go wrong. However, there are a few criteria that can be used on the last round that will usually lead you to the correct play. First of all, realize that if you bet on the last round it should be for one of two reasons:

1. To get a better hand than yours to fold, or
2. To get a worse hand than yours to call.

If you don't have a decent chance of accomplishing either of these objectives (as in the four jacks hand) then you should not bet.

Even if you think, however, that a bet will be profitable, it still doesn't mean that you should do so. It still may be better to check if you are not last to act, if this does better in the long run. An obvious situation would be if you can check raise with a good hand. Less obvious would be cases where you should check and call even if you think you have the best hand, and even if you think you might get called, if you bet. A check is better if you now may entice him to bluff, especially if your check also induces him to bet those hands worse than yours, that he would have called with. This play also avoids a raise. For instance, suppose you make

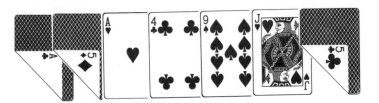

on seventh street in seven-card stud and are looking at what appears to be a pair of kings and a straight draw. It may be better to check and call if

1. You're quite sure he won't call with just kings,
2. He will bet kings-up or better if you check, and
3. He might bluff if you check.

For a fuller treatment of last round play see my book *The Theory of Poker*.

# Odds For a Backdoor Flush

Let's work out the odds that you need to get from the pot when all you have is a "backdoor" flush draw. The answer may surprise you. Suppose, for instance, that you are holding

(playing hold 'em) and the flop comes down

Your only real chance is if the next two cards are both spades. (There is a small chance that you could win without a flush, and a small chance that you could make a flush and still lose. However, these two eventualities are unlikely and tend to cancel each other out, so they will be ignored in this analysis.)

It should be obvious that you wouldn't even consider calling a bet on the flop unless the pot was huge. How huge must it be? If you were playing $10-$20, would it be worth calling a $10 bet if the pot already contained $200? What about $300? The answer depends on a few factors. One factor, of course, is whether you can be sure that there will not be a raise on the flop. If you have to call a second $10, the calculation goes out the window. Thus, for this analysis, I will assume that you are almost positive that it will cost you only one bet on the flop and probably one bet on fourth street to try to make your flush.

So, what are the chances of making a backdoor flush? In the example that I gave in which you hold 10♠9♠, you start out by realizing that there are 10 unseen spades remaining out of 47 unseen cards, so the probability that the fourth card is a spade is simply 10/47. Now, if it is a spade, the chances that the last card also will be a spade is 9/46. The chances that both cards will be spades is, therefore, these two numbers multiplied together or 90/2,162.

$$\frac{90}{2,162} = \frac{(10)}{(47)}\frac{(9)}{(46)}$$

This means that you will make your flush (on average) 90 out of 2,162 tries or 4.163 percent of the time.

$$4.163\% = \left(\frac{90}{2,162}\right)(100)$$

If we think in terms of odds, we see that in 2,162 tries, we fail 2,072 times for every 90 times that we succeed, so the odds are 2,072-to-90, which is about 23-to-1.

$$2,072 = 2,162 - 90$$

$$23.0222 = \frac{2,072}{90}$$

Now, many experienced players know this number, and they proceed to call $10 on the flop as long as there is $230 or more in the pot. Many good players don't require even quite this much in the pot, since they reason that future possible bets won, when they make their flush allow taking a short price now. *However, there is a flaw in this thinking.* This is because they forget to take into account the extra $20 that they will lose when the spade comes on fourth street but not on the end. This will happen with a probability of 370 out of 2,162 times.

$$\frac{370}{2,162} = \frac{(10)}{(47)}\frac{(37)}{(46)}$$

(Please stop reading if you don't see how I got this. It's not hard. Just slowly reread everything.)

Now, to fully analyze this hypothetical $10-$20 example, we take into account this extra $20 that is sometimes lost, as well as the extra money that is won when the backdoor flush is made. This extra money won is at least $20, and probably more. To put everything together, we first separate things into three cases:

1. In 90 out of 2,162 times, you win the pot plus at least $20.
2. In 370 out of 2,162 times, you lose a total of $30 after the flop when the first card off gives you "false hope."
3. In the remaining 1,702 out of 2,162 times, you lose $10.

Therefore, in these 2,162 hypothetical trials, we need our 90 winning hands to make up for our losses of $10, 1,702 times, and $30, 370 times, which is $28,120 worth of losses.

$$\$28,120 = (\$10)(1,702) + (\$30)(370)$$

In order for our 90 wins to make up for this, we have to average $312 profit per backdoor flush.

$$312.44 = \frac{28,120}{90}$$

There has to be $292 in the pot on the flop to guarantee a $312 profit, including the fourth street bet. If you can count on another $20 on the end, the after-flop pot can be as little as $272 to make a call barely worth it. However, even with these optimum assumptions, we still need about 27-to-1 odds on the flop rather than the simplistic 23-to-1 that most players accept. (It is worth taking 23-to-1 only if you or your opponents are all in or if you don't expect a bet on fourth street.) When you add in the fact that you might have to call a raise somewhere along the line, the truth is that backdoor flush draws that have no other outs are hands that almost always should be dumped, except in those rare cases in which you are getting more than 30-to-1 odds.[9]

---

[9]It is important to understand that backdoor flush draws are valuable when you have other things going for you. Add in a backdoor straight draw, small pair, or even just an overcard, and you have a totally different situation in which even 10-to-1 odds may be worth taking.

# When Time
# is Not of the Essence

One of the concepts that I introduced many years ago was that of "hourly rate." I stressed that if you were trying to make a living by playing poker, it was important to think about how much you would average per hour in a particular game. Then you would go ahead and put in the hours in those games that figured to yield a good hourly rate, without worrying about how you were actually doing. In the long run, your profit should be close to your hourly rate multiplied by the number of hours played. Your only concerns would be to find the best game, and to play in such a way as to give you the highest possible hourly rate.

When I first wrote these ideas, few players were thinking of their "poker business" in quite these terms. Even most pros were too concerned with having winning sessions rather than simply putting in the hours and playing their best in good games. Nowadays, however, there is a large contingent of professional players who think and play exactly along these lines. It is, of course, clearly the right way to think, especially if you are grinding out your income in approximately the same size game, day in and day out.

There are, however, some instances in which maximizing the hourly rate is not necessarily the best play. These exceptions are valid even when analyzed from the standpoint of logic and mathematics.

To give an extreme example, let's say that a complete sucker challenges you to a heads-up, $5,000 freezeout, no-limit hold 'em match. Furthermore, this is all the money he has. You, on the other hand, have a $40,000 bankroll that you have accumulated at a $50 per hour rate from the day-to-day casino games. You gladly accept his offer, even though you don't think he will give you a rematch if he wins.

Now, you can play this game in two different ways. You can gamble with him a little, finish the match in about two hours, and have an 80 percent chance of winning. Or, you can drag the match out to about five hours by playing very carefully, thus increasing your chance of winning to about 90 percent. Your mathematical expectation for the longer match is $4,000, but it's only $3,000 for the shorter match. Clearly, it's worth dragging out the match three extra hours for an extra $1,000 in expectation, since those three hours would have made you an average of only $150 in other games. However, had you been thinking purely in terms of hourly rate for the match, you would have chosen the short-match strategy, as this gives you an hourly rate of $1,500

$$1,500 \; = \; \frac{3,000}{2}$$

rather than $800 for the longer match.

$$800 \; = \; \frac{4,000}{5}$$

Of course, the above example was very hypothetical, and I used it only to illustrate the principle irrefutably. In real life, it never is quite so clear cut. However, I will give some examples of situations in which you might consider playing more cautiously than theoretically optimal, as far as managing your hourly rate is concerned.

1. You are in a game with one or more wild players who must eventually go broke, and none of the other games in the room is worth nearly as much.

2. You are in a very good game, but you have a short bankroll and cannot continue to play if you lose more than a certain amount.

3. You are in a game in which some of your opponents play badly when they are big losers but play well otherwise. If they do get badly stuck, it is unwise to gamble with them with only a small edge, if this risks getting them even.

4. You are in a game with some bad players who will quit if they get ahead a certain amount. It is similar to the previous example, in which you should not build up the pot in those situations if winning will make the sucker quit.

In the above situations, you most likely would consider playing with a strategy other than the optimum hourly rate strategy when the alternative games in the room are much worse. Of course, the best example of this is when you are in a private game and have no place else to go anyway .

# Dealer Abuse

I have something to say about dealer abuse. This is a common occurrence in the bigger games. Players sometimes throw cards at the dealer, insult him or her, or declare that they will never tip. Sometimes this happens because the dealer made a mistake. More often, it is because the dealer dealt the abusing player a losing hand.

While I never have knowingly abused a dealer, I have a confession to make — I like it when I see someone else do it! It's not because I am a sadist, and it's not because I secretly wish that I had the gumption to do it myself. Rather, it is because I am delighted to know that my opponent is an imbecile!

The fact is that any player who gets mad at the dealer for his losing cards truly is a complete moron, and his stupidity ought to make me money. Yes, there are some successful players who fit this description, but they almost always are the ones who happen to instinctively play one game well. It is very rare to see the top all-around players (who are almost always the most intelligent) act this way. So to repeat one more time, if you don't think the dealer is cheating, and you still abuse him or her when you lose, you simply are an idiot.

However, there is more to say before the dealers cheer my words. What about dealer errors? Of course, even this is not justification for flagrant abuse, because of the simple fact that such behavior is simply not nice and wrong under almost any circumstances. (Also, I think it is gutless on the part of cardroom management to tolerate this from the high-stakes players while the same actions from a lower-stakes player, would doubtless result in him being barred, at least temporarily.)

However, there are some players who, while they are not extremely abusive, do give dealers a very hard time when they make even the smallest error. Are they going overboard? Yes, they usually are and I will explain why in a moment. First, however, let me tell you about the one time that even I get mad. It is when the dealer is being obviously careless (such as dealing out the next round before all the bets have been called.) Often a player, upon seeing such carelessness, will say something like, "What are you doing, dealer? Don t you realize that we are playing $100-$200 here? Of course, it's not your money, so what do you care?" I agree with the sentiment. The fact is that I think dealers should concentrate hardest in the bigger games. Ideally, of course, it would be nice if they kept up their concentration in all the games they dealt, but few people are capable of that. Occasionally, the mind drifts to automatic pilot, but every effort should be made to prevent this from happening while dealing the bigger games. It happens because I think some dealers assume that the money is of the same relative value to the players in all sizes of games, but this isn't true. The players in the big games almost always are gambling a much higher proportion of their net worth than those in the small games. The smaller-game players usually are playing for fun. That's not so for the bigger players.

Still players who get very irritated at dealers for small, infrequent mistakes are wrong (with the exception just noted of obvious dealer carelessness). The reason has to do with a syndrome that I have noticed in many settings. It usually occurs in the business world in the form of a CEO or entrepreneur becoming abrasive toward subordinates when they are not perfect. (I know some casino owners who fit this description.) I have come to realize that their abusiveness stems from the fact that to *them*, the error that caused their tirade seems easily avoidable and clearly unacceptable. They know that if they were doing the job, they would not have made that mistake. What they fail to realize is that they have risen to their position of prominence because they are different than most people. They should not judge others by their standards. If those others had their standards, they wouldn't be working for them.

The same is true with high-stakes professional poker players and dealers. I recently heard a pro player telling a dealer that he himself could do a better job. *Of course he could,* but so what. Expert poker players usually are gifted with astute minds that could be used in many endeavors. Dealing certainly is one of them. However, those who actually deal probably do not have the alternatives that the pro player has. If they did, they probably would pursue them. (I realize that I am now losing most of the points I gained with dealers earlier in this article, but so be it. The purpose of my writings always will be, first and foremost, to illuminate the truth.) So those players who are nasty to dealers for every trivial error, with the justification that they are not meeting the same standards that they would meet if they were dealing, are being needlessly mean.

# Comparative Advantage

I suppose some readers may think that I was being "inflammatory" in an earlier essay when I said those players who abuse dealers for dealing them losing cards are morons and imbeciles. Maybe I misspoke. I should have said they were nitwits and idiots. As for my comments about players who are needlessly harsh to dealers about trivial errors because they know they themselves could do a better job, I wrote this not because I wanted to put down dealers. Rather, I was interested in introducing a concept that really deserves its own essay. Namely, the principle of comparative advantage. The general idea is that you should delegate some tasks to others even if you are better at these tasks than they are, since you have more important fish to fry. Not doing this can be very inefficient. (It even may be right to delegate the more important fish if you are far superior at frying the other fish, but only slightly better with the big fish. This actually is a precise mathematical concept that is applied normally to world trade.) However, once you do realize the need to delegate this way, you should not get angry when a job is not done quite as well as you could do it. Anyway, I used dealers and players to illustrate this principle simply because they were the most convenient.

Before leaving the subject of dealers, I ought to say a little about tipping. Obviously, tipping based on whether you won the pot and how much was in it is a contrived way to tip. However, it has become the accepted procedure. One logical way to tip if you are a regular player is the following: Tip in such a way that if everybody tipped similarly, the dealer would make a reasonable amount for the day. For instance, if a dealer deals about 150 hands per day, you might think that he or she ought to average about 75 cents per hand dealt. If so, you might want to make this your average tip, depending on the size of the pot. You know that tourists frequently tip more, while others tip not at all, but that is not your concern. No dealer should complain about you if you use this method.

Furthermore, if you are trying to make a living by playing poker but are just struggling along, it should not be expected that you toke off a high percentage of your income. You still are helping dealers indirectly by keeping games going.

# An Essential
# Hold 'em Concept

You are playing $10-$20 hold 'em. You are dealt

You raise. A tight player reraises. You reluctantly call, knowing that she is almost certainly holding a pair of aces, kings, queens, jacks, or AK suited. The flop comes down

You have two aces, but you don't like it, as you know that 3 of her 5 possible hands (AA, JJ, AK suited) have you beaten and almost drawing dead. But you should like it, as your chances of having the best hand are not 40 percent, but are, in fact, 60 percent. I'll show you why in a moment, but first let's look at a second example.

You raise with

A player reraises. This player is similar to the one above, except that he will do it with AK off suit as well as AK suited. You now make the interesting play of reraising to find out whether he has aces. When he just calls, you put him on KK, QQ, JJ, or AK. Now the flop comes

2 of his possible hands beat you and 2 of them don't, but you are far from even money. In fact, you are a 3-to-1 favorite (75 percent) to have the best hand.

Many experienced hold 'em players are very adept at narrowing down their opponent's probable two-card hands quite precisely. Unfortunately, most of these players misuse their information when trying to decide the chances that they have the best hand, especially after the flop. There are three reasons for this:

1. Some two-card hands are more likely to be dealt than others.
2. The chances that an opponent has a particular hand changes after you take into account the cards you are holding.

3. The chances that an opponent has a particular hand changes after you take into account the cards in the center of the table.

The general method that should be used when assessing the probability of the various possible hands that your opponents might hold, is to come up with the number of combinations of cards that could make that particular hand, and compare that with the number of combinations of cards for the other possible hands. For example, if you have seen no other ace, the number of combinations of cards that can make up a pair of aces is 6 (A♣A♦, A♦A♥, A♣A♠, A♦A♥, A♦A♠, A♥A♠). The same would hold true for any other pair. For a specified suited hand, there obviously are 4 combinations. AK suited could be any 1 of the 4 different suits. Any AK can be made up in 16 different ways. You get this by multiplying the 4 possible aces by the 4 possible kings. The same goes for KQ, J10, or any two-card, nonpaired hand. There are 16 ways to be dealt each of them if none of those cards are exposed. (Since 4 of those combinations are suited, there are, therefore 12 combinations that are unsuited.)

So if you know that a player has either aces, kings, or AK, realize that he is more likely to have AK than the other 2 hands combined. More specifically, his chance of having AK is 16 out of 28, or 4/7, or about 57 percent.

Do you see why? It is because there are 16 ways of being dealt AK compared to 6 ways each for AA or KK. Thus, if you know that he has 1 of these 3 hands, there is a total of 28 combinations, 16 of which are AK.

What about when you see a relevant card either in your own hand or on the board? How does that affect the probabilities? Well, it can affect them dramatically. To give an extreme example, let's say that you know your opponent holds either a pair of aces or a pair of kings. Now the flop comes down

He has, therefore, aces-up or quads. It is simple to see that it is 6-to-1 against four-of-a-kind. This is because there is now only 1 combination remaining of two kings, while there still are 6 available combinations for two aces. For a less obvious example of the same math, suppose that you hold

the flop comes

and you once again put your opponent on a pair of aces or kings. As before, his chance of having two kings in the hole is 6-to-1 against (or 1 out of 7), since the two kings that you've accounted for leave him with only 1 combination.

Let us now see exactly how seeing 1 or more relevant cards reduces the number of combinations that can make up a possible two card hold 'em hand. In the case of pairs, the 6 possible combinations decreases to 3 if one of them is seen elsewhere, and, of course, goes down to 1 combination if 2 of them are seen. For nonpairs, the idea is to multiply the number of available cards of each rank. With no cards seen, that is (4)(4) or 16 combinations. Take 1 card away and you have (3)(4) or 12 combinations. Other possibilities are (3)(3) = 9 or (2)(4) = 8, and so on. In the case of suited hands, use common sense. If you see an ace, there are 3 remaining possible combinations of AK suited. If you also see a king, there are now 2 remaining combinations of AK suited, *unless* the king is the same suit as the ace, which would still, therefore, allow 3 AK suited combinations.

Now let's get back to the examples with which I started this essay. In the first example, I said that you have A♥Q♦ and you know that your opponent has either AA, KK, QQ, JJ, or AK suited. When the flop shows A♣J♣4♥, it is time to start counting combinations. With 1 ace in your hand and 1 on board, there is only 1 combination left for her to hold two aces. However, there still are 6 ways available to her to have two kings. This is not so for two queens, as there is a queen in your hand. 3 combinations remain for that. So far, we have counted 9 combinations that she can hold that you beat, and only 1 that beats you. What about a set of jacks? With the jack on board, there are 3 ways she can hold two jacks. The score is now 9-to-4. Finally, what about AK suited? With 2 aces seen (1 on board, 1 in your hand), there are only 2 AK suited combinations left. So the total number of combinations that she can have that beats you is 6 (assuming our assumptions about her possible hands were correct). Meanwhile, you beat 9 combinations that she can have. So your chances are 9 out of 15 (or 9-to-6, or 3-to-2, or 60 percent) that you have the best hand.

*Please notice, however. that if we had included all AK combinations among her possible hands, that would have given her a total of 8 possibilities for AK [(2)(4) = 8]) rather than the 2 that we gave her. A small adjustment like this would give her a total of 12 winning combinations vs. the same 9 losing combinations. This would bring your best hand chances down to about 43 percent.*

*Thus, you can see why accurate card reading is very important in hold 'em.*

In the second example, you flop a set of eights when it comes K♠Q♦8♥, and you put your opponent on KK, QQ, JJ, or any AK. If you have been paying attention, this problem should be easy. There are three ways he could have a set of kings. The same goes for queens. However, there still are 6 ways he could hold two jacks. As for AK, there are 12 combinations remaining (4 aces times 3 kings), so of the 24 combinations that he can have, only 6 beat you. You should win about 3 out of 4.

I am going to leave you with one last example, but I won't give you the answer until the next essay. It's not difficult, and it comes up quite frequently. Please try to do it yourself.

This time, the play has made it obvious that your opponent has a big pair, jacks or better, an AK of any type, or AQ suited. You hold

The flop is

What's the chance that you flopped the best hand?

# More Hold 'em Essentials

In the last essay, I left with you a problem that I hope you tried to work out yourself. You held Q♠Q♥ (playing hold 'em). You knew your opponent held aces, kings, queens, jacks, any AK or an AQ suited. The flop came Q♣J♥T♦. What were the chances that you held the best hand?

Obviously, the only way he could have you beaten is if he held an AK. In the previous essay, I showed you that there are 16 possible combinations of this hand when no other aces or kings are seen, so there are 16 combinations of cards that he could have had that beat you. Other possibilities that he could have had are AA (six combinations), KK (6 combinations), JJ (3 combinations — because a jack is showing), and AQ suited (1 combination — because there is only 1 queen left).

Adding these up (6+6+3+1), we get 16. Thus, there are 16 combinations that beat you and 16 combinations that you beat. You are only even money with your top set to have the best hand. (It should be pointed out that you actually are a small favorite to wind up with the best hand when the smoke clears. This is because when he does flop a straight, you have about a one-third chance of drawing out. On the other hand, when you flop the best hand, his chances of drawing out are less than this, on average. His best hope, of course, is when he has two kings.)

I am not quite done with this subject. So far, I have used mainly esoteric examples to show the results of using math to read hold 'em hands, and I have specified precisely the possible hands that your opponent could have. This was necessary because, unfortunately, there can be major swings in the odds that he has a particular hand after the flop when his starting hand requirements change only slightly. To show this, let us compare two hypothetical players. Player A will raise with AA, KK, QQ, JJ, AK, or AQ. Player B will raise with these same hands plus AJ.

121

Now let's suppose that you have

and the flop is

Against player A, there are 21 combinations that beat you — AA; KK; QQ; JJ; and AQ — while there are only 12 AK combinations that you beat (for now). Your hand should be frequently folded in this spot. Against player B, however, everything changes. Because there also are 12 combinations of AJ that he can hold, you are now a 24-to-21 favorite instead of a 21-to-12 underdog.

The effect may be even more pronounced if the flop is something like

Player A still has 18 combinations to beat you. Adding 6 combinations for two jacks to the 12 combinations for AK results in 18 combinations that you beat. So this flop has improved your chances, but only to about even money against player A. On the other hand, you are now a big favorite against player B, since you have added 16 combinations of AJ to his possible holdings. You are a 34-to-18 favorite because of that.

However, you cannot always assume that just because someone will play (or raise with) more starting hands, that it always increases your chances of having the best hand after the flop. For instance, using the above two hypothetical opponents again, let's say you have

and the flop is

Against player A, he beats you with 17 of his possible combinations — AK; AQ; AA — while you beat 18 of them — KK; QQ; JJ. So you actually are the favorite. However, against the guy who also could have AJ (player B), you turn into a 25-to-18 underdog.

After seeing what the addition or subtraction of just one hand like AJ can do to your assessment of an opponent's hand after the flop, you can imagine how much things change among varying opponents who might or might not play quite a number of starting hands. No wonder it is so important to be able to read hands in hold 'em. No wonder it is so important to know the math after you read the hands. And no wonder those who can't do both will lose to those who can.

# Comparing Ace-King
# to Ace-Queen

How much better is AK than AQ as a starting hand in limit hold 'em? It turns out that the answer is that it is quite a bit better. The difference between these two hands probably is greater than you think. One way to show this is to analyze the following scenario. A tight opponent raises before the flop You put him on having a big pair (jacks or better), AK, or AQ. Everyone else folds and you have to decide whether to call him with your hand. The question is, what are your chances of winning (or tying) if you have AK? What about AQ?

We are going to assume that somebody is all in or almost all in, which means that both players will get all five cards. However, not assuming this would change the results only slightly.

First, let's say that you have AK. That means that there are 3 different ways that he can hold AA. The same is true for KK. However, there are 6 ways he can hold QQ or JJ. There also are 9 ways that he can have AK and 12 ways that he can have AQ.

To summarize:

### If You Hold Ace-King

| Opponent's Hand | Number of Combinations | Percent of Total |
|:---:|:---:|:---:|
| AA | 3 | 7.7% |
| KK | 3 | 7.7% |
| QQ | 6 | 15.4% |
| JJ | 6 | 15.4% |
| AK | 9 | 23.1% |
| AQ | 12 | 30.7% |
| Total | 39 | 100.0% |

Now let's assume that this situation comes up 1,000 times. This means that he has aces about 77 times, kings about 77 times, jacks or queens about 154 times each, AK about 231 times, and AQ about 307 times

So in these 1,000 hands, you will have about 769 hands that don't figure to be pushes.

$$769 = 1,000 - 231$$

How (approximately) will you do in these 769 hands? It works out like this:

Of the 77 hands he has aces, you will win about 5.
Of the 77 hands he has kings, you will win about 23.
Of the 308 hands he has queens or jacks, you will win about 140.
Of the 307 hands he has AQ, you will win about 220.

Again, these figures are approximations. In any case, we see that of the 769 hands that you have that are different than his, you will win about 388 This is approximately half. In other words, against a player who will raise with a big pair, an AK, or AQ, your AK is about even money to win.

Now, what about AQ?

### If You Hold Ace-Queen

| Opponent's Hand | Number of Combinations | Percent of Total |
|:---:|:---:|:---:|
| AA | 3 | 7.7% |
| KK | 6 | 15.4% |
| QQ | 3 | 7.7% |
| JJ | 6 | 15.4% |
| AK | 12 | 30.7% |
| AQ | 9 | 23.1% |
| Total | 39 | 100.0% |

Again, there are about 769 hands out of 1,000 that don't figure to be pushes. Here's how you will do in these 769 hands.

Of the 77 hands he has aces, you will win about 5.
Of the 154 hands he has kings, you will win about 45.
Of the 77 hands he has queens, you will win about 23.
Of the 154 hands he has jacks, you will win about 70.
Of the 307 hands he has AK, you will win about 87.

Thus, with AQ, you will win only about 230 of the 769 hands that you don't push. This is only about 30 percent.

This example should make it clear why there are many times that you should play an AK, but not an AQ.

# A Cute Hand

People are always asking me whether poker is more mathematics or psychology. The fact of the matter — as any poker expert understands — is that the best players not only use both disciplines but also know how to combine them. Here are a few simple examples with at least one result that may surprise you.

Say you're playing hold 'em. You raise before the flop with

A tight player reraises. You know this player so well that you are sure he has a pair of aces or kings in the hole. You call, hoping to flop a set. The flop comes

What are your chances of having the best hand? Think before answering.

I hope you didn't say even money. If you did, it's probably because you figured that since he was equally likely to have aces or kings it is now even money that he has three kings. But there is a flaw in that thinking. It has to do with the fact that a king showing on board now makes it more likely that your opponent holds two aces. More precisely, there are six different combinations of two aces that he could hold (A♥A♠, A♥A♦, A♥A♣, A♠A♦, A♠A♣,

A♦A♣) but only three combinations of two kings now that a king has shown. So it is a 2-to-1 favorite that your three sevens is the best hand.

What if there are two kings on board (as well as your seven)? How scared should you be? The answer, of course, is not too scared, since it is now 6-to-1 in favor of your opponent holding aces-up. There are still six combinations of two aces but only one combination of two kings left for him to hold. If the five cards on board were miraculously

do you see that you are a 3-to-1 favorite? Think about it.

Now let's see if we can apply similar techniques to seven-card stud. This hand actually happened to me. I raised with a queen. A tight player reraised with a five showing. Since I knew that he would slowplay three fives, I was sure he had aces or kings in the hole. Anyway, by fifth street he had two kings showing. On seventh street I had four queens. On the end he bet, I raised, and he reraised. I was sure this reraise indicated a monster hand of at least kings full or aces full. So how likely was I to be beaten by four kings? (I purposely did not go into the details of how the hand was played in the middle betting rounds so as not to muddy the waters of this essentially pure math problem.)

Players who are somewhat familiar with the mathematics concept shown in the previous hold 'em example will see an analogy and assume that four kings is far less likely to be his hand. Mathematically unsophisticated players will also expect a full house to be much more likely simply because they are virtually always more likely than quads. But they are all wrong!

This is not completely analogous to the hold 'em problem. Yes, it is true that on sixth street it is six times as likely that he had aces and kings as opposed to four kings.

But there is a new factor here that didn't exist in the hold 'em situation: If he did have only two pair he has now filled up! Since he will fill up only 10 percent of the time, the fact is that it is more likely that he has four kings than that he had aces-up and then filled up.

To show this simply, say that this situation (having aces or kings in the hole and showing two open kings) occurred 700 times. Six hundred times he would have aces-up on sixth street and 100 times he'd have four kings. All well and good. The kicker here is that of the 600 instances he has two pair he will fill up only about 60 of those times. So of the 160 times that he reraises, in about 100 of those he has four kings and in about 60 he has a full house. In other words, about 63 percent of the time he raises on seventh street he has four kings.

# Is Your Wallet Fat Enough?
### Calculating your daily maximum swing and bankroll requirements for playing in a limit poker game.

Aspiring professional poker players always have two big questions for me — both related to money. Number one on the list: "How much of a bankroll do I need to ensure that I don't go broke if I play a particular limit?" And number two: "How many hours must I play before I can trust that my results accurately reflect how I really ought to do?"

The answers are interrelated. And of course the subject has been investigated and written about before, principally by Mason Malmuth. In an effort to be accurate, however, Malmuth, who was once a professional statistician, uses formulae and nomenclature that a good many players don't want to deal with. The good news is that I have come up with a way to explain these concepts so anyone can understand without sacrificing too much precision.

Good poker players will win a certain amount of money per day on average. However their results for any particular day will not always be even near this average amount. For instance a $6-$12 hold 'em player who figures to win $80 per day in the long run may well find himself a $500 winner or loser after a six-to-eight hour session. In other words, there will be major swings from his average on any particular day. The term I've coined for this is "max swing" — it's simply the maximum amount that you can expect to deviate from your average earnings for a particular period of time on all but the craziest of periods. Interestingly, estimating your max swing for a day is a lot easier than estimating your average daily win. The reason is because your max swing is not related so much to how well you play but rather to the size of the game and how much action there is. Tight players have lower max swings than loose players, but even their max swings go up in a wild game.

In any case, in my experience the max swing in most games is somewhere between 75 and 100 big bets for an eight hour session.

Getting back to that $80 a day $6-$12 player, this means that his daily max swing would be around $1,000. So he can expect a daily result of somewhere between minus $920 and plus $1,080 the vast majority of the time. (The max swing theoretically swings around his daily average. Thus his results will be $80 plus or minus $1,000.)

Don't forget we are talking about typical six-to-eight hour sessions here. Other games would have different daily max swings. For a tight $10-$20 game it might be $1,400. For a loose $75-$150 stud game with a large ante it might be $15,000.

So how do you use this concept of max swing? Let's go back to that $6-$12 player whose average win is $80 a day but who sometimes swings from that result by as much as $1,000. Let's suppose he plays twenty-five days (and puts in about the same number of hours per day. If, for instance, he played two short days you would combine them into one for these purposes). How should he be doing after all these sessions?

Well, we can expect him to be up about $2,000 since (25)($80) = $2,000. But this is just an average. One lousy day can swing as much as $1,000 remember. So after twenty-five days could his results be as much as $25,000 different from what you would expect? This would make his outcome range from being a $23,000 loser to a $27,000 winner. That seems farfetched and is in fact wrong. You *do not* multiply the max swing from one day by the total number of days to get your max swing for the whole period. Rather you multiply the max swing for one day by *the square root* of the number of days in question.

So in this case the max swing for twenty-five days is $5,000. You get this by multiplying $1,000 times the square root of 25 which is 5. Our $6-$12 player's twenty-five day result will be $2,000 plus or minus $5,000; in other words he will range from a $3,000 loser to a $7,000 winner.

You can estimate your max swing for any number of days even if you don't know what you can expect to average winning per day. All you need to know is that your max swing for any number of days is your daily max swing times the square root of the number of days in question. After one hundred days our $6-$12 player could have results that are $10,000 off from what they should be. (1,000 times the square root of 100 is 10,000.) He might still be as much as a $2,000 loser when he should expect to be an $8,000 winner.

Put another way, his results could be off in either direction by as much as $100 per day or $13 per hour even after three months. After four hundred days his max swing from his expected results is $20,000. Notice, however, that this is now only $50 per day or about $6.50 per hour. So after four hundred days this $80 daily winner should be ahead about $32,000 and almost certainly will be winning between $12,000 and $52,000.

It's most helpful if you do all these calculations for yourself. Even if you don't, however, here is a rule of thumb anyone who is keeping careful track of his or her results can use: It will take at least a year before you can be quite sure that your hourly rate results are accurate to within one small bet. A $15-$30 player who is ahead $10 an hour after a year may actually be a losing player (or up to a $25 per hour winner). However, someone winning $35 after a year can be sure he can beat the games, if maybe only for $20 an hour.

Some of you may find it discouraging that it takes a year or more before you can expect your experimental results to be a fairly accurate prediction of what's in store for you in poker. On the other side of the coin, three months playing should give accurate results to one big bet per hour and even three weeks playing should not be off by more than two big bets per hour. In other words, if you are winning three big bets per hour after three weeks you can be almost sure that you are a winning player, and conversely if you are losing three big bets per hour after three weeks you can be almost sure that it's not just bad luck.

So just what is the required bankroll for a professional poker player? Notice that as the days wear on both your expected profits and your (total) max swing go up. But they don't move up at the same rate. Your daily expected win is multiplied by the number of days you play, but your total max swing is arrived at by multiplying by the square root of the number of days. Let's look in again at our $6-$12 player with the average $80 daily win and a daily max swing of $1,000. What are the worst results he could have? These are shown in the table below.

**Worst Possible Results For an $80 a day $6-12 Player**

| Number of Days | Worst Results | |
|:---:|:---|---:|
| 1 | (1)(80) - (1)(1,000) = | -$920 |
| 4 | (4)(80) - (2)(1,000) = | -$1,680 |
| 9 | (9)(80) - (3)(1,000) = | -$2,280 |
| 16 | (16)(80) - (4)(1,000) = | -$2,620 |
| 25 | (25)(80) - (5)(1,000) = | -$3,000 |
| 36 | (36)(80) - (6)(1,000) = | -$3,120 |
| 49 | (49)(80) - (7)(1,000) = | -$3,080 |
| 64 | (64)(80) - (8)(1,000) = | -$2,880 |
| 100 | (100)(80) - (10)(1,000) = | -$2,000 |
| 144 | (144)(80) - (12)(1,000) = | -$480 |
| 169 | (169)(80) - (13)(1,000) = | +$520 |
| 225 | (225)(80) - (15)(1,000) = | +$3,000 |
| 400 | (400)(80) - (20)(1,000) = | +$12,000 |

What you can see happening here is that our $6-$12 player at first needs a larger and larger bankroll to withstand his worst possible results — but only up to a point. Since he is a winning player there comes a time when his expected win should overcome his max swing to the point that it is virtually impossible that he would be losing. In the above scenario, this should occur somewhere between 144 and 169 days. More importantly there should occur a point much earlier than this where the maximum needed bankroll has reached its peak. According to this chart, it looks like this happens somewhere between 36 and 49 days and it looks like the needed bankroll never gets past $3,200. And that is indeed the case.

There is a simple formula that can be used to calculate the required bankroll you'll need to guard against going broke.

(Assuming that you do not reduce your stakes when you are losing and you do not take money out of your bankroll for expenses.) The formula is:

$$Required\ bankroll = \frac{(Daily\ \max\ swing)^2}{(4)(Daily\ average\ win)}$$

This means that you take your one-day max swing, multiply it by itself, divide by 4, and finally divide by the average daily win. For our $6-$12 player this is $3,125.

$$\$3,125 = \frac{(1,000)(1,000)}{(4)(80)}$$

This is the required bankroll. A $75-$150 stud player who averages $400 a day and has a daily max swing of $15,000 needs $140,625.

$$\$140,625 = \frac{(15,000)^2}{(4)(400)}$$

Notice how dependent your bankroll requirements are on your average daily win. If we increase our $75-$150 stud player's average daily win to one big bet an hour ($1200 for an eight hour session), his bankroll would only have to be $46,875.

$$46,875 = \frac{(15,000)^2}{(4)(1,200)}$$

Of course all of the foregoing assumes that the quality of the games are not changing too much — nor is the quality of your play. It also assumes that you are estimating your expected daily win accurately. When you estimate everything correctly, and have the bankroll indicated by the preceding formula there is only a 3 percent chance of going broke due solely to bad luck.

That's the main reason to know these formulas. They allow you a lot of leeway. If you ever need more than the formula says you should, you can be almost sure that you are lying to yourself about how much you can win.

# Is Your Wallet Fat Enough for Tournaments?

How big a bankroll a professional poker player ought to have to guard against going broke is a good question — and one I just analyzed in the preceding chapter. But we were talking about regular poker games. Tournaments are another animal. Since I am writing this at the time of the World Series of Poker, it's appropriate to do a similar analysis for tournament players. In other words, what kind of financial cushion does a person need to play poker tournaments as a business? (This question of course assumes that the player has the best of it, i.e., a long-run edge. If the player isn't one of the favorites in the tournament, no amount of money will do.)

Figuring out the required bankroll for a tournament player is far more complex than coming up with a dollar amount for someone playing regular poker games. We can't use simple calculus and simple formulas as we did for the regular game situation. But there is another way: namely, to use a computer to simulate the life of a tournament player. With this in mind I contacted Wayne Russell, a superb computer programmer and developer of the computer game *The World Series of Poker Adventure* (which is now produced by Masque Publishing.) He and I also collaborated on the *Hold'em Freezout* video game, so I had the utmost confidence that Wayne would be able to carry out the simulations accurately.

I told Wayne to assume that our hypothetical player played a multitude of tournaments with the following parameters:

**Buy-in:** $1000 + $35 entry fee
**Number of Entrants:** 200

## Prize Structure

| Place | Amount |
|-------|--------|
| First | $80,000 |
| Second | $40,000 |
| Third | $20,000 |
| Fourth | $12,000 |
| Fifth | $10,000 |
| Sixth | $8,000 |
| Seventh | $6,000 |
| Eight | $4,000 |
| Ninth - Twelfth | $3,000 |
| Thirteenth - Sixteenth | $2,000 |

Of course, most tournaments do not have this exact buy-in or structure. Therefore the results would have to be adjusted for different parameters. (Instructions for how to do this are at the end of this essay.) For now, however, let's look at this specific tournament structure.

First, notice that the total prize money is $200,000 (which equals the total of the buy-ins). The casino keeps the $7,000 in entry fees and returns the rest. If you played two hundred such tournaments and finished in each one of the money positions exactly once, you would have invested a total of $207,000 and gotten back $200,000. So you would be down $7,000 or $35 per tournament. But this assumes that you are only an average player. What happens if you are good enough to get into the money twice as often as the average? In other words, suppose in a tournament such as this you figure to win one in one hundred times (rather than one in two hundred) and finish second once in one hundred and so on down to sixteenth place. If you are this good you figure to get back $200,000 in prize money (after a hundred tournaments) while investing only $103,500.

$$\$103,500 = (100)(\$1,035)$$

Your expected net profit is therefore $96,500 or $965 per tournament.

$$\$96,500 = \$200,000 - \$103,500$$

$$\$965 = \frac{\$96,500}{100}$$

Clearly a player of this caliber ought to be playing in these tournaments. And there are a few players who are this good. So I had Wayne simulate a player like this on his computer. (He also simulated a player who hits each money position once in 150 times. We will get to that shortly.)

Remember, however, that these one in one hundred figures are just averages or probabilities. A player could play hundreds of tournaments without winning any. What the computer did was have a player play a thousand tournaments and record the results. Then, it had a second such player play a thousand tournaments, then a third. Altogether the computer had a thousand different "players" with a 1 percent chance for each money spot play a thousand tournaments each.

So what are the results of the thousand expert players playing a full schedule of $1,035 buy-in tournaments for a dozen years or so? Well, the good news is that they were all in the black when the smoke cleared. And on average they won over $900,000 as expected. But one guy was only $110,000 ahead or $110 per tournament. Fifty players won $500,000 or less. This means that there is about a 5 percent chance that you will be winning less than half of what you should be winning after playing a thousand tournaments! And it is even worse if you are not as expert as these hypothetical players.

Another interesting statistic is the number of tournaments these players had to play before finally breaking into the black for good. One player didn't get out of the red for good until the 684th event.

This great player was still behind after many "years." Fifty players needed more than 175 tournaments to reach the black for good. So there is about a 5 percent chance that you will need more than two years of steady tournament play to get ahead and stay ahead, even if you play this well.

Which brings us to the key question: bankroll requirements for a tournament player (not including expenses). Well, in the million-tournament simulation there was one player who found himself down $130,000 at his worst point. Fifty players were at times down more than $55,000. Thus, if you play as well as these guys there is a 95 percent chance that $55,000 (about fifty-five buy-ins) will be an adequate bankroll and a 5 percent chance it won't. If you have a smaller bankroll, it would be wise to sell "pieces" of yourself.

For those of you who don't rate yourselves as highly as the above hypothetical players but still think that you are a favorite, we did the same simulation assuming the player hits each money spot an average of once in 150 tournaments. This still gives you a nice theoretical edge. After 150 tournaments you will have invested $155,250 and gotten back $200,000 on average. So you figure to be up $44,750 after 150 events or about $298 per tournament.

$$\$155{,}250 = (150)(\$1{,}035)$$

$$\$44{,}750 = \$200{,}000 - \$155{,}250$$

$$\$298 = \frac{\$44{,}750}{150}$$

(Notice that this is a far cry from the $956 profit for the one in a hundred in-the-money player.) When these guys and gals played through their tournament career on the computer, fifty-nine were still losing after a thousand tournaments! It's obvious that you can't truly count on making a living playing tournaments at this skill level, especially if only the top 8 percent of the players get into the money as is the case in these hypothetical events.

As far as bankroll requirements for these very good but not great players, 5 percent of the computer players were down more than $130,000 at some point. So if you want a 95 percent chance of surviving in tournaments like these you will need a cushion of about 130 buy-ins plus living expenses — which is about 2.5 times what the great player needs.

The bottom line result for players on the "tournament tour" seems to be that great players need about 55 buy-ins and the very good players need about 130 buy-ins to feel fairly safe. Furthermore, the merely very good player needs some luck to make it, and even great players can have a two-year dry spell. However, this assumes that the tournaments you play in are similar to the one simulated (i.e., two hundred players and sixteen money placers) *and* that your chances of finishing in each of the money spots is about equal. Changing some of these factors could change your bankroll requirements.

For instance, if there were fewer entrants in our hypothetical tournament it would be harder to run unlucky and you would need less of a cushion. Likewise, if there were more money places. Either of these changes would result in more than 8 percent of the entrants getting something back. If the tournament was not weighted as heavily to the top three spots this would also lessen bankroll requirements. Another factor is your playing style. You may have the same long-run positive expectation as another player but you place in the top three more often, while he is more likely to make it to the final table. This makes your results more volatile so you need more money. So, if the tournaments you play in are a lot different from the one the computer played, you may want to adjust its results a little.

For most tournament players, however, the conclusion is simple: Going through 40 buy-ins probably doesn't prove anything about you and tournaments, but going through twice that probably does.

# Questions and Answers

**Question:** I have been playing Texas hold 'em for about two years, but I seem to be losing money with one particular class of starting hand: ace-rag suited. Could you please comment on the value of this hand in general in loose games? Should I call in early position knowing a raise is probable before the flop? How about calling a double bet cold in late position?

I would also appreciate your analysis of the following scenario:

I defend my big blind against the preflop raiser to my immediate left (there were six cold calls, so I'm getting 15-to-1 with no possibility of a reraise behind me) with

The flop is

Should I bet or check? Assuming I check and the pot gets bet and raised, do I call the double bet? If, for whatever reason, I am in there on fourth street and a diamond falls that does not pair the board, how much heat should I now take to try to make the nut flush?

**Answer:** Taking your questions one at a time:

1. Ace-rag suited is normally not that good a hand and should be frequently thrown away, especially in early position. It's better in loose games as are all mediocre hands that have a decent chance of making the nuts.

2. The hand is rarely worth a double bet unless you were against five or more opponents (Of course, if you have already called a single bet, you are now forced to call a raise.)

3. You should probably bet your A♦2♦, mainly because you will have to call if someone else bets. It is usually better to be the bettor than the caller, plus you may have it the best hand.

4. If you check and are facing a bet and a raise you are getting about 10-to-1 odds from the pot. Your chances of catching a deuce, a four, a five, or a backdoor flush are enough to justify a call. However, this is all the more reason to bet

5. If you catch a diamond that doesn't pair the board, you should call even a triple bet cold in the situation you have described. You will still be getting more then the required 5-1 odds.

**Question:** Although relatively experienced in regular games, I am new to tournament poker. One of many questions is how to play with short stacks since I never even come close to going all-in in a regular game. For example, I believe I made a mistake with a short chip position in the later stages of a small hold 'em tournament. There were two tables left with six players at each table. This tourney pays the top four finishers in proportion to how many chips each player has remaining once the final four is reached. Anyway, I was on the button with only eleven chips left and had to post an eight chip small blind. The pot had already been raised from early position by a good player and there was one call of the raise by the

time it was my turn to act. I held

and threw my hand away. In retrospect it seemed that in this position any hand (even 7-2 offsuit) was worth going all in with. What would be your recommendation in this situation? In addition, any other general advice on trying to survive with short stacks in tournaments would be appreciated.

**Answer:** When a tournament pays the top finishers in proportion to the amount of chips they have in front of them, your strategy should be almost identical to what it would be in a regular game. Thus, you should call for three chips more after posting an eight chip blind with any two cards. It is conceivable (though not likely) that you would want to save these three chips if the prizes were awarded differently.

**Question:** I was playing in a $3-$6 hold 'em game. It was a good game with a few tourists playing too many hands. I was in the big blind ($3). First position just calls (a tourist who is a *calling station*); everyone else folded. The small blind called. I know how the small blind plays; he would have raised with any kind of good hand. I figured him a small threat. The tourist in first position was exposing his hand to me unknowingly. I saw that he had the

I had the

The flop came

Here is my question. I came out betting — knowing he would only call but hoping the small blind would also call. He called; the small blind folded ($15 in the pot. The turn was a blank. I figured that knowing what he had justified taking the short price on pot odds. I had eleven outs. I bet; he called ($27 in the pot). The river was a blank. I checked; he bet; I folded. If a diamond or a jack comes, I figure to make $39 total (my bet and his call). What are your thoughts on this situation?

**Answer:** I am sorry to say you made quite a few mistakes on this hand. First, you should have raised before the flop regardless of whether or not you saw the tourist's hand.

Secondly, you should have checked on the flop and let the tourist bet. If the small blind called, you would raise. If he didn't call, a raise is still okay.

And finally, you have 14 outs, not 11. In spite of this you should check on fourth street since there is no chance that you can make the tourist fold.

**Question:** The following situation occurred when clinging for survival in a small hold 'em tournament. The limits were $200-$400 and I had $300 left. The other seven players have at least $1,000 each and the prize money doesn't become significant unless you finish third or better. I was in the big blind for $200 and was dealt a

Another player who appeared to be solid raised from first position and everyone else folded. Is it correct for me to go all in with my last $100 chip? It seems to be a good play since I could be blinded out next hand anyway, and I was getting 6-1 pot odds on my last $100 chip. I'm writing since the play was criticized by a player who has a lot more experience and tournament wins than I.

On the other hand, if the situation occurred in a ring game with both players having plenty of chips and the raiser was tight and aggressive, would it be correct to fold?

**Answer:** Yes, you were correct to call with your K♣9♥, getting 6-to-1 odds. The only hand he could have where it wouldn't be worth it for you to call would be two kings.

If you are in a full ring game and a tight player raised in early position and you have plenty of chips you should fold. You should also make this fold even if he is not very tight.

**Question:** Let's say I have a good seat in a decent $10-$20 hold 'em game in a large Southern California card club with eight other players. There are a few fairly loose players on my right. The two solid, aggressive players are sitting on the opposite side of the table. To my left are players who could be classified as "weak-tight." There are no maniacs (i.e. constant rammer/jammers) in the game. My question concerns the play of small pairs (deuces through sixes) before the flop. There seems to be more than the usual disagreement among expert poker analysts as to what is the correct strategy. I would appreciate a critique of my current strategy and reasoning. The question is divided into several parts, depending on position and players who have already acted as follows:

1. I'm on or next to the button with a small pair. No one has called. Is it correct to mostly raise (sometimes fold), hoping either to get one-on-one with a single blind, or to steal the blinds? (Note: I will usually try a steal with a variety of other marginal hands.)

**Answer:** Always raise.

2. Once again, I'm on or next to the button with a small pair. One or two players have called. Is it correct to mostly fold because the odds against hitting trips compared to the pot and implied odds are too great, and you can't steal because of the original callers?

**Answer:** Call, unless there is a strong possibility of a raise behind you. The implied odds are there.

3. I'm in late position with a small pair. Three or four players have already called. Is it correct to almost always call (occasionally raise) hoping to hit trips?

**Answer:** Yes.

4. Again, I'm on or near the button with a small pair. Five or six players have already called. I often raise (sometimes call) because the pot odds, compared to the odds against hitting trips, seem to justify it. (This assumes the original callers will call my raise and probably one of the blinds.)

**Answer:** Correct.

5. One last time, I'm on or next to the button with a small pair. There was an early raiser and three cold callers. This could be the pot of the night! Is calling correct, or is the danger of set-over-set too great?

**Answer:** It's close, but you should not worry about set over set.

6. For number five above, would it be correct to occasionally reraise?

**Answer:** No.

7. In early position (first three in front of the blinds) with a small pair, is it correct to routinely fold (except for calling from third position if the first two positions call)?

**Answer:** Call if you expect callers, but not raisers, behind you.

8. In early position with a small pair, if the game is weak and very loose, is it correct to call?

**Answer:** Yes.

9. I'm in a middle position (dealer and one or two others yet to act) with a small pair. If there have been two or more callers in front, is it correct to call? I reason we should pick up a couple more callers and even if it is raised, there should be at least four-way action.

**Answer:** Correct.

10. Once again, I'm in a middle position with a small pair. If there has been only one caller so far, is it correct to usually fold (except when the caller is a bad player)? My reasoning is that you probably can't steal; the hand is too weak to raise with; and there is not enough likely action to justify seeing the flop, hoping for trips.

**Answer:** It's close.

11. One last time, I'm in middle position with a small pair. No one has called. Sometimes I call, hoping for several more callers; other times I raise, hoping for a steal or a one-on-one with a blind; and sometimes I fold. I figure I may be unsure of my play but at least I'm deceptive! Any comments?

**Answer:** It's close between calling, raising, and folding.

12. I'm in the big blind with a small pair. A tight player in early position raised. Everyone else folded. Is it correct to usually call?

A: The answer to this question depends on how *well* the raiser plays from that point on. You should fold against top players in this situation.

**First question:** Normally, I play in the $10-$20 hold 'em games at the large card clubs. They all have a small blind of $5 and a large blind of $10 to the left of the dealer button. In *Hold 'em Poker For Advanced Players* you address this structure and it has helped me tremendously. Unfortunately, the weekly tournaments use a structure that adds a small $5 blind to the button. Could you explain some of the implications of this blind? I am primarily interested in how this affects "steal" plays both on and near the button. This seems particularly important because you often get a chance to steal the blinds in tournaments since play is usually much tighter than in open play.

**Second question:** In your first hold 'em book you strongly make the point that any hand that can call a raise cold is strong enough to raise with. I wonder if the following before-the-flop situation is a valid exception to your point. You have a hand like

on or near the button. There were several early callers and the player to your right raises. You call, figuring the original callers will call the raise and you will have five or six way action for what could be a big hand. If the pot hadn't been raised you would only occasionally have raised yourself. Does this logic appear to be correct? If so, could you provide better examples of exceptions to your rule?

**Third question:** There seems to be some disagreement concerning whether and when it is correct to rebuy in tournaments. So far my tourney experience is limited to about 20 events. I have had many decent finishes, including several trips to the final table; however, my entry fees currently exceed prize money won. Since I enjoy tournaments and want to gain more experience, I have budgeted an average of $150 a week for entries. I'll spend more only after tourney play proves to be profitable. There are about six weekly tournaments I could attend with entry costs ranging from $40 to $49. You generally receive either $150 in chips with limits starting at $10-$20 or, $100 in chips with limits starting at $3-$6. All give you the same ratio. This does not count the house fee which applies only to the original buy-in and ranges from zero to $9. Despite the fact that there is no fee on a rebuy, my philosophy is never to rebuy unless I run out of chips early in the first round and I'm at a weak table. Since I'm currently limited to an average of only three buy-ins per week, I figure it is best to enter another tournament. If I get eliminated, regular games are also available. Do you think this philosophy is appropriate or correct for someone in my situation?

**Answer:** In reference to question one, there are two conflicting aspects to there being an extra blind on the button. There is more money in the pot and thus more money to "steal." However, it is less easy to get away with it. This second point is the more important one, so bluffs and semi-bluffs should be tried less often when you are to the right of the button. On the other hand, it is now critical to raise with your good hands as you don't want to let the button play for only half a bet.

Referring to your second question, your example may not be an exception. A reraise may still be worth it, especially if it will knock out the early callers and result in all that "dead money" in the pot. An exception would occur if the raiser was early and he got several cold callers. Now you can just call also.

As for your third question, rebuys are usually, theoretically correct, even late in a tournament when you are one of the best players. However, this does not take into account the fact that if you are eliminated, you could be playing in a profitable side game. So I don't disagree with your approach.

**Question:** I have been playing hold 'em for approximately a year. During this time I have yet to learn how to handle a series of "bad beats." I am unsure whether the best tactic is to change seats or to quit for a short period of time. Also would you recommend changing seats if the seat I am in is "cold?"

**Answer:** If a series of bad beats rattles you to the point where you feel that you are not playing your best, it may be wise to take a short break to regain your composure.

However, cards are random. Your luck cannot be changed by changing seats or taking breaks. If you are losing in what is clearly the best seat (based on how your opponents play) you should stick it out in that seat. If, however, there is a good strategic reason to change seats (such as being to the left of a "live one") then by all means do so. In fact, it might be a good idea to change seats when you are losing even if the new seat seems strategically the same as the old one. There just might be something about your old seating position which is contributing to your losing that you haven't discerned. So a change wouldn't hurt.

**Question:** I seem to do very well playing $3-$6 and $5-$10 limit hold 'em as long as everyone is playing kind of tight, but when I play in what I consider a "great game" where everyone is playing every hand, I always get clobbered; they always out draw me.

Is there a different strategy that should be employed in one of these crazy games?

**Answer:** As Mason Malmuth and I explain in *Hold 'em Poker For Advanced Players,* there is a different strategy necessary to take optimum advantage of a wild and crazy game. It has to do with placing more importance on hands that can make *monsters* (even if it's a longshot) compared to good hands that do poorly against

many players. For instance,

is a better hand than

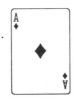 

in a game like this. A small pair and a backdoor flush draw is usually playable on the flop. Big draws should be pushed hard as you are usually getting great odds from your multiple opponents.

Conversely, high pairs should be played in such a way as to knock out as many opponents as possible. This is usually done by raising or check-raising the player on your right. If you can't do this, your hand is probably only worth a call.

**Question:** I play quite a few of the small ($15-$25) buy-in tournaments in Las Vegas — mostly hold 'em. I'd like your advice on starting-hand requirements after the rebuy at the $50-$100 and $100-$200 limits when players have tightened up considerably — but many short stacks are going all-in by raising with hands anywhere from good to bad!

Also assume your chip position is moderate to weak ($600 to $800) at the $50-$100 limit and $800 to $1400 at the $100-$200 limit). Also how aggressive should you be after the flop with hands like

or

when playing against a similar stack of chips as yours, against one other player if the flop hasn't helped your hand?

**Answer:** The key to playing a moderate stack in a tournament when the limits have moved up is to be the bettor or raiser but not the caller. Since your opponents are trying to protect their chips, you should loosen up a little before the flop if no one else is in yet. Never just call the blinds if no one else has called. Either raise or fold. However, if someone else is in, especially if they have raised, fold all but your best hands and reraise with most of those. In other words, loosen up your semi-steal raising requirements but tighten up your calling requirements compared to a regular game.

After the flop the same applies. Be more willing to bet but less willing to call than in a regular game. The exception to the above occurs when you are against short stacks who have just about given up. If they are playing recklessly, you have to be prepared to call them.

**Question:** The game is $2-$4 hold 'em at my regular cardroom. There are two blinds — the dealer puts in $1, the man (or lady) to the left puts in $2. I am the dealer and hold a

suited. Three players call in front of me, I call. The big blind does not raise. The flop is

There are five players who have seen the flop. The blind bets $2. Three players call. Should I call? Please give a detailed reason for your answer.

**Answer:** You should fold. Though you are getting 9-to-1 pot odds, it's still not worth taking a card off with this hand against four other players. You almost certainly do not have the best hand. So you have to catch 1 of 5 cards to improve (2 jacks or 3 eights). The odds against doing this are about 8-to-1 which might seem to indicate that the hand is worth a call. The problem is you can improve but still lose. It is likely that someone else has a jack (probably with a bigger kicker) so this brings you down to three cards to hit. And there is no guarantee that jacks and eights will win. So calling is clearly wrong even without a two flush on board. (If a two flush was showing, calling would be insane.)

**Question:** While playing a stud tourney, I had a

on my first three cards. Another player had an ace up and raised before the action got to me. Since it is common to raise with an ace in that position (often to steal the antes), I called. My next card was a king; the raiser's an ace. Open aces bet. I folded three kings. (The player showed his three aces.) I assume I did the right thing? What are the percentages of either one of us filling for a full house?

**Answer:** While your play *turned out* to be right for *that hand*, it was actually wrong. If you thought there was a good chance your opponent did not have two aces to start with, you should be even more skeptical that he has trips when another ace shows. It is inconsistent that you could call on third street with the idea that you very well may have the best hand and then fold on fourth street when you both pair your door cards as this *increases* your chances of having the best hand. (The only exception would be if you knew your opponent would be too timid to bet into your open kings unless he could beat three kings.) As to the actual hand in question, both of you are a little less than 40 percent to help your trips. You would therefore beat him about 1 in 4 times if you played to the end. (40 percent that you improve times the 60 percent that he doesn't equals 24 percent.)

**Question:** I'm in my first year of playing poker on a regular basis. I play $1-$4-$8 hold'em with a $1 blind. I thought this would be a good level to start at.

I have taken your advice and play tight, but aggressive. I think my image at the tables is just that. This approach sometimes gets me into trouble. The weaker and intermediate players, and particularly the tourists, won't bet their hands. They are intimated by my play. They will check and call, or just call, often with the best hand.

My question is as follows: *Is there something I can do better to ascertain what they have and still maintain my aggressive style?*

**Answer:** Your question is a very good one. The problem you are having is much more common than you think. It is a problem experienced frequently by journeymen pros when they drop into smaller games.

First you must understand why tight, but aggressive play is usually the correct style in the bigger games against the better players. It is because these players are capable of folding mediocre hands when you bet. You can bluff or semi-bluff them out on later rounds because they know that your initial starting requirements make it likely that you have a good hand.

If, however, you were aggressive but not tight, good players would take advantage of you by letting you bet their hand for them. They would rarely show any strength, preferring instead to let you bet your money off with hands you might have thrown away had they bet or raised.

Thus, you see that when you play so aggressively against weak players you scare them out of betting their legitimate hands. You have forced them into a correct strategy (of a sort) against you.

A very tight and very aggressive strategy is actually not correct against weak players, especially in a game like the $1-$4-$8 hold 'em game where you can see the flop cheaply. For one thing you shouldn't play all that tight. Against bad players, playing tight won't set up bluffs as they will against good players. More importantly, you miss opportunities to make big hands that will beat bad players out of a lot of chips.

As far as aggressiveness is concerned, the key is to be aggressive on an early round with your mediocre hands, but then give yourself a free card on the later rounds, rather than bet a hand that very well may not be the best hand. These free cards and saved bets are the best way to take advantage of your opponents' meek play.

**Question:** The ring game I usually play is 50-100 FIM (Finnish Marks) spread limit with 25/50 FIM blinds, 5 percent max of 75 FIM rake and a maximum of four bets per betting round in a multiway pot. The opponents I play are in general pretty loose, with a couple players being very aggressive, but most quite passive. Usually there are a couple of 100-200 split limit experts in the game too. Before the flop I play much slower and much tighter than in split limit; I for example don't play even medium suited connectors from even middle position. However, I play pairs in the split limit games. After the flop I check raise less and slowplay more in the unraised pots. I was wondering if these are the right adjustments and if there is anything else I can do in order to optimize my way of playing for this kind of spread limit game? Almost forgot, my bankroll is short, only 200 big bets.

**Answer:** I am not sure what you mean by spread limit. If you mean that you can bet 50 to 200 at anytime including before the flop your present play is essentially correct. You cannot play marginal hands in middle or early position if there might be a big raise behind you. This is doubtly true because of the large rake you are facing and because of your limited bankroll. In fact, if you are playing pairs below eights in this position you should stop.

On the other hand if 50 is the maximum bet before the flop you can play small pairs and suited connectors because of your high implied odds and the fact that you can only be raised 50 FIM. Even in the other structure these hands can be played when there is little preflop raising.

You are right to slowplay more often on the flop when the pot is small. But it still should be a fairly rare play.

**Question:** I would like to know your thoughts on how to play both AK suited and unsuited, pre flop on the button in both a loose passive and loose aggressive game when there's no raise to you and when there are raises to you. If your answer depends on the number of callers, does the big blind count as a caller?

**Answer:** With AK suited (on the button) always raise or reraise regardless of the situation.

With AK offsuit (on the button) if no one else has raised in front of you raise unless there have been five or more callers in which case you should sometimes just call. If there has been a raise in front of you, you should just call unless you think a reraise will get the pot heads-up. If there has been a raise and a reraise in front of you, you should fold if the reraiser is a tight player.

In aggressive games you should be more apt to just call before the flop in the hope that this will encourage someone to bet into you. If you flop an ace or a king you can now raise and limit the field.

# Part Two

# Life

# Logical Decisions

In these essays, I will have something to say about things that are going on in the world or things that are being said, that are simply wrong. I say this not for egotistical reasons but rather because I will usually only bring up something if I see a logical flaw. *My subjects pick me — not the other way around.* By this I mean that I will rarely write about something simply because it interests me. Rather it is only when I hear or see something illogical that I jot down an idea. Thus, I am more likely to say something having to do with people with black skin rather than girls with freckles, even if I'm more interested in the latter category. It is of course, possible that there will be flaws found in some of my arguments. But that does not mean that I am expressing an opinion. Rather it means that I have miscalculated somewhere. If I say that someone has added up a column of numbers incorrectly, I may be wrong, but the fact remains that there is only one right answer.

It turns out that there are many issues in the real world that similarly have a right answer, especially if you frame the question properly. In other cases there may be more than one answer but *not* if you have agreed to a previous stipulation. (Example: If you agree that it should be illegal to allow a premature baby to die if it could be saved by an incubator, then you must agree that a fourth month abortion should be illegal 300 years from now when the technology could save such fetuses. But you need not come to this conclusion if you don't accept the first premise.)

It is a sad fact that people are constantly getting confused about things especially when it takes a knowledge of logic and/or probability to reach the right answer about something. Let us take the general idea of making a decision between two alternatives when the results of that decision are in doubt. Who should I vote for? Should I marry Karen? Do I fire John? Do I hold the concert indoors to protect against rain? Do I paint my house white or black?

Even to the non-mathematicians these are clearly problems that have something to do with probability. And to most it would appear to be a simple matter of choosing the alternative that will more likely turn out right. That might be hard to do, but it seems that if you can do it you now have found your best choice. This may seem obvious, but it is not necessarily correct. In other words the best choice is not always the one that has a higher probability of turning out right. There are three ways this can happen:

1. The choice with the higher probability of being right has a small chance of turning into a disaster, but the other choice doesn't. For example, if there is a 20 percent chance of rain and your indoor auditorium holds almost as many seats as the outdoor stadium it may be better to sell a bit fewer tickets to the concert rather than take a chance on having to give everyone a refund.

2. The choice with a lessor chance of being better has a small chance of offering giant rewards while the first choice doesn't. Thus I may elect to keep the irresponsible but creative John to design my newspaper ads because he just might come up with a blockbuster.

3. If I pick the alternative with the greater probability of being the better one I am stuck with it, but the same is not true for the other choice. If I'm not sure whether I'd rather have my house painted white or black (and I suspect I'd prefer black) I should still try white first. Now if I don't like it I can paint black over it but not the other way around. Likewise if I think I prefer Jane but she will wait for me and Susan will not then you ... well, you get the idea.

# What Makes
# an Issue Controversial

I would like to analyze what it is that makes an issue controversial. It is not simply that the issue is important. Rather, it is the nature of the arguments surrounding it.

It is easiest to see what I mean by visualizing a balance scale that is perched atop a standard-type scale. Now assume that this balance scale is weighing the arguments for one side of an issue on its left platform while weighing the arguments for the other side on its right platform. Using this analogy, I contend that controversial questions have a few precise properties, the first and foremost being that the scale is precariously balanced.

This first property should be obvious, because if one side of the scale clearly outweighed the other side, only a small minority of people would stubbornly ignore the relative weights of the arguments to continue to espouse the "wrong" side. And when a large majority of people agree on the correctness of a side, we have no controversy. However, if the arguments on both sides have nearly identical weights, then advocates for both sides realize that it takes very little to tip the balance.

However, a precariously balanced scale normally is not enough by itself to make a question controversial. It also is necessary that the total weight of the scale be large. This doesn't necessarily mean that there are many arguments on both sides, because all arguments do not weigh the same. Some are much "heavier" than others. For instance, in the abortion issue, there is only basically one argument for the "right to life" side, but many believe that this argument outweighs all other arguments that may be on the other side.

There are two reasons·why controversial issues almost always involve a heavy balance scale. The first is the fact that most people will not get too riled up over an issue involving only "lightweight" arguments, even if they see it as a close decision and even if they disagree with the outcome (unless, of course, they are personally involved). An example might be the question of "colorizing" old movie classics. Another example might be who would make the best mayor of your town. In these cases, the balance scale may be horizontal, but the whole scale doesn't weigh much. Only issues causing a heavy scale get the widespread attention that is necessary for them to be truly controversial.

The second reason why a heavy scale is much more likely to inflame passions actually is unfortunate. It has to do with the fact that many people are unwilling to objectively compare both sides of an issue. For these people, if the side they champion carries heavy weighted arguments, that is enough for them, regardless of the weight of the arguments for the other side. Therefore, when the whole scale is heavy, there will be plenty of people of this ilk to fan the flames for their own particular side. (I hate people like this, by the way. They are the ones who cause most wars.)

Thus, we see that most controversial questions involve a precariously balanced balance scale that itself weighs a lot.

There is frequently another factor as well. Continuing with the scale analogy, the fact is that many high-profile, emotional, controversial issues get that way because the proponents of one side or the other disagree with the weight of the arguments involved, even if they admit their validity. This comes up most frequently when the points for both sides involve unrelated factors. The typical case is when one side is for a principle and the other side is for pragmatism. Should we give out clean needles to drug addicts? Should prostitution be legalized? Should there be forced busing to achieve integration? Should we use the medical knowledge gained from the horrible Nazi experiments in the concentration camps? In cases like these, people on one side of an issue usually are willing to admit the other sides points — they just don't agree on their weight. Questions like these are thus, almost impossible to resolve.

# The 95 Percent
# Criterion Fallacy

Beta carotene doesn't prevent cancer. Coffee doesn't cause it. Betting against pro football teams that played the previous Monday night will not show a long-run profit (laying 11-to-10 odds). These are all apparently true statements. But all three were once considered to be false. Why is it that we constantly hear new theories about medicine, vitamins, or other things based on learned, well prepared studies from major universities which turn out to be wrong when the smoke clears?

The problem is that medical researchers and the media frequently use flawed reasoning. The culprit is the so-called 95 percent confidence limit, which is the general criterion most researchers and journalists employ before they will print a surprising result or theory. But this method of testing a hypothesis has problems that any good gambler should be able to recognize — and guard against.

The so-called 95 percent confidence limit criterion works like this: If researchers are performing an experiment to test a new hypothesis (such as "coffee causes cancer"), they will only accept this hypothesis if their results had less than a 5 percent chance of occurring under the old hypothesis. So, for example, let's say in a typical group of 100 people there is only a 3 percent chance that more than 15 of them will develop diabetes. We now hypothesize that Dr. Pepper causes diabetes. We check this out by having 100 subjects drink two bottles of Dr. Pepper per day. If 16 of them develop diabetes, we accept our hypothesis, write it up in the *New England Journal of Medicine,* and cause a stir in the soft drink community.

We feel we have a right to condemn Dr. Pepper because there is only a 3 percent chance that we would get these results if Dr. Pepper has no effect on diabetes development. (Remember: There is only a 3 percent chance that more than 15 out of 100 people, under normal circumstances, will develop diabetes.) So researchers point the finger at Dr. Pepper as the reason that more than 15 people develop diabetes — because there is only a 3 percent probability of this occurring, due to chance alone.

But this is *not* the same thing as saying that there is only a 3 percent chance that Dr. Pepper is innocent. Yet people constantly confuse the two statements. It annoys me that even doctors and journalists aren't generally aware of this trap that they frequently fall into.

To illustrate this confusion more clearly, suppose I proclaim that painting coins green results in far more heads than tails when they are flipped. You test this idea by painting a quarter and flipping it five times. You get five heads. This will only happen by chance 1-in-32 times or about 3 percent of the time. But it is obviously absurd to conclude that there is only a 3 percent chance that my theory is wrong (that painting coins results in more heads) and a 97 percent chance that I am right. That is not what these results say. These results merely describe the random results of a coin toss.

When statisticians and experimenters need only to satisfy the 95 percent confidence limit criteria before making a big deal about their results, something screwy happens. Suddenly 1 in every 20 experiments yields "statistically significant" results that seem to show something unusual or important — but in actuality, all that it shows are simply random results where nothing special is going on. Now combine this point with the fact that there are 10,000 or so experiments carried out every year. There will be a few truly important breakthroughs and insights gleaned from these experiments — but there will also be about 500 results that pass the 95 percent confidence limits yet portray findings that are simply due to chance and are thus *completely wrong*. Yet these results are frequently published under banner headlines until further studies eventually refute them.

There are two ways to reduce (but not eliminate) this problem. One way would be to insist on much tougher confidence limits, say 99.5 percent. The second method is to consider how plausible the new hypothesis is, based on factors other than purely experimental results. (To do this more precisely requires something called Bayes' Theorem as explained in my book *Getting the Best of It.*) More plausible theories should not require confidence limits as high, before experimental results supporting them should be taken seriously. Less plausible theories should require higher confidence limits.

If you notice that you usually win when you get ten hours sleep the night before you play, you are probably being scientific when you make a connection. If you notice that you win after you take a particular beautiful brainy redhead out to dinner, I think your theory may just be romantic.

# Coincidences

We saw in the previous chapter that many apparently "newsworthy" results of experiments or studies are in fact merely coincidences. But there's a flip side of this issue. Namely, many apparently incredible coincidences probably aren't coincidences at all. To illustrate this, I will use Bayes' Theorem in a way I have never seen it used before. In fact, I'd like to hear from professional mathematicians or statisticians on the subject of whether or not I have in fact discovered a new application for this theory.

Here's the general idea: if there are incredible coincidental events that seem to be unrelated but just might be related after all, then I would bet that they are related. For instance, if Los Angeles experienced a major earthquake immediately after a snowstorm, I would bet it wasn't a coincidence — this, in spite of the fact that there is no obvious connection.

The math works like this: let's say geologists think there is a 1 percent chance that snowstorms trigger earthquakes and a 99 percent chance that they don't. If we assume that a major earthquake happens once every thousand days in Los Angeles and that a snowstorm happens once every thousand days, then there will be a snowstorm and an earthquake in L.A. only once every million days if there is no connection. Put another way, no connection means a snowstorm/earthquake day is a one in a million shot. But a 1 percent chance of a connection makes a snowstorm/earthquake day a one in a hundred-thousand shot. Thus, it is about a 10-to-1 favorite that a snowstorm/earthquake day was not a pure coincidence, even though geologists started out by thinking a connection between these two things was a 99-to-1 underdog. (I am oversimplifying here. For instance, geologists might believe that there is a 1 percent chance that a snowstorm will result in a 50 percent chance of an earthquake. With these figures a snowstorm/earthquake day is about a 5-to-1 shot to not be a coincidence.)

Now the above was a hypothetical, contrived example used principally to illustrate the basic idea and the math (although I did notice that two earthquakes I experienced followed major rainstorms). But there are plenty of real life examples. Here are five of them; the first two we now know weren't coincidences — the last three I would bet aren't coincidences either.

1. *The Space Shuttle exploded the first time it was launched in below freezing weather.* When the Space Shuttle Challenger tragically exploded in 1986, I was sure there was a connection even though the experts at first denied it. After subsequent investigation, however, NASA determined that the frigid conditions affected the O-rings on the shuttle leading to the explosion.

2. *The Oklahoma City bombing was the same date as the Waco fiasco and the Randy Weaver incident.* When authorities first arrested a man of Jordanian heritage, I was sure they had the wrong man. Sure enough, it soon became clear that the bombing that resulted in hundreds of deaths, including children in a day care center, was not the work of Arab terrorists as police originally hastily concluded, but instead was a retaliation for Waco. Police later arrested two members of a white anti-government group who had been scouting government buildings and amassing explosives.

3. The world's smartest man (or close to it) has lived with Lou Gehrig's disease longer (or close to it) than anyone else with the disease. I speak, of course, of Stephen Hawking. I can't believe this is a coincidence. Somehow his brain keeps him alive. I hope medical science investigates further.

4. There is a man who will always make the correct call when you flip a coin and catch it in your hand. He somehow has the ability to see the coin even as it is twirling. This man is a real person. This man also is afflicted with Tourette's syndrome (a very rare disease involving uncontrollable tics). My Bayes' theorem technique says an unknown connection is far more likely than a

coincidence. Perhaps there are readers out there with this syndrome who might want to check out their coin-seeing ability (or something else involving seeing things in apparent slow motion) and get back to me. If I'm right, this is also something medical science should investigate.

5. A man drops a glove at a murder scene and though he gets rid of everything else, he drops the *other* glove at his house *and* the cop who finds it spent years making tapes about how he plants evidence. By no means am I saying that O.J. Simpson is innocent. But I sure wouldn't mind taking about 4-to-1 odds that he didn't bring that glove home.

The bottom line is that you can use probability to show that incredible coincidences with an unlikely connection probably aren't coincidence after all. Of course, to do this, the unlikely connection must be at least plausible. If an earthquake followed the Rams shutting out the 49er's, you would have to call it a coincidence — even if that event is as unlikely as a snowstorm in L.A.

# Will Power

Note: This essay is also in the "Poker and Gaming" section of this book.

It often is thought that one of the main reasons for my success as a poker player is the fact that I don't steam or "go on tilt" when I am losing. In point of fact, the ability to keep from steaming is not nearly as important as the ability to choose games and play well. It is true, however, that you must do better in the long run if you always are playing your best and choosing good games, regardless of whether you are winning or losing. Despite this obvious fact, not steaming is easier said than done. So, how do I do it?

It is important to understand that playing your best or quitting a bad game when you are stuck actually is an act of will power, the same kind of will power that you need to stay on a diet, quit smoking, or start an exercise program. What is happening in all these cases is that you are trying to put up with some discomfort today in order to gain even greater rewards in the future. In the case of poker playing, the discomfort is the bad feeling that you get when you go home a loser that evening. The only way to have a chance at alleviating that feeling when you are badly stuck is to play a lot of hands that you shouldn't play, in a desperate attempt to get even for the day. That strategy usually will backfire, of course, but occasionally it works. If you play your normal, solid game, you can hope to recoup only a portion of your losses, and the bad feeling remains.

Of course, getting back some of your losses adds that much more to your eventual profits, if you are a winning player. Since the ability to accept the lousy feeling of a sure loss today for even greater rewards in the future is a mark of will power, we see that not steaming is, in fact, a test of will power.

I have come up with a few techniques to develop my own will power. They ought to work for you, also. First, 1 realized that there is a big difference between thoughts and feelings, and in the short run, feelings take precedence. Therefore, my idea was to make my feelings rather than my thoughts give me will power.

One way to harness your feelings to give yourself will power is to take great *pride* when you stick to a resolution, and to feel great *shame* when you don't. Make yourself feel that sticking to your resolution is more important than the subject matter of that resolution. If you can develop this attitude, you will have will power without having to resort to logic to talk yourself into playing well or exercising. You do it because it feels worse if you don't. *Make yourself feel more pain from letting yourself down than the pain you feel by exercising or losing, and your emotions will keep you on the right course, automatically.*

A second way to harness your own emotions to give your will power strength is to realize that time is merely a dimension. Physics tells us that, and it's true. Time is just another way of specifying where we are. If I gave you $1 million and, simultaneously, transported you to Australia, you would still be happy in spite of your changed location. You should feel the same about time.

Three months from now, you would rather have $67,000 than $65,000, even if it meant one extra losing day three months earlier. Six months from now, you would rather be thin than fat, even if it meant some hungry days leading up to it. So the key to this technique is to think of the rewards of your will power not occurring in the future, but simply at another place. (The only drawback to this way of looking at things involves incidents from your past. For those incidents that were good, this philosophy makes it easier to relive and savor them. However, when they were bad, or when someone has wronged you, it is not true that "time heals all wounds." It would make no more sense to forgive someone who has made no amends, simply because four years have gone by, than it would to forgive him the next day simply because he moved to Australia.)

Anyway, time is only a dimension, and the ability to visualize your greater happiness in the future, just as if it were happening in another place, cannot fail to help your will power to do the right thing.

# Risking Your Life

There was a book printed many years ago with a title something like *Strategy in Poker, Business, and War.* I do not remember the name of the author, nor did I read the whole book, but I do remember that the general subject matter was game theory. The fact is that tactical and strategic decisions as far as how to conduct a war frequently can best be arrived at by using the same principles that should be used to analyze games. However, there is one big difference between games and wars. In wars, people die.

Now I'm not just being cute here. The fact is that people dying in a war screws up the game theory analysis. (Most people also think that people dying in a war is wrong for religious or moral reasons. Others think that it is OK morally if the cause is just, but these are personal opinions and I don't get into such things. It is hoped that my points will be agreed to by all thinking persons regardless of their personal beliefs.)

To show why risking death cannot be put into gaming terms, let us imagine ourselves being asked to take a small risk of something horrible in order to gain something beneficial. For instance, let's say that you know that if you call in sick from work, you will be able to beat a guy who is in town only one day out of $1,000 playing gin rummy. However, you know that if your boss catches you, you'll be fired, and that's not worth $1,000. You estimate your chances of being caught at only 1 percent. So, is it worth taking a 1 percent chance of getting caught to pick up $1,000? That depends on you and your situation, but if your answer is yes, then your answer also should be yes to the question of whether you would take a 2 percent chance of getting fired for $2,000, and a 10 percent chance for $10,000. They all have the same *mathematical expectation,* and if you answered yes to all these questions, game theory says that you should simply allow yourself to be fired if you were paid $100,000. Now this makes perfect sense. If you are not willing to take $100,000 to be fired, you shouldn't take a one in 100 chance of

173

being fired to gain $1,000. (An argument can be made against this idea by using something called utility theory, but it would rarely apply, and I mention it only so that the discerning reader doesn't think that I overlooked it.)

It should be obvious, however, why this same type of analysis falls apart when you are risking your life rather than money, fame, happiness, or injury. Would you take a 1 in 1,000 chance of dying for $25,000? If yes, does that mean that you would take a 1 in 100 chance for a $250,000? Even if you said yes again, I doubt that you would let me flip a coin to see whether I kill you or give you $12.5 million, and I know that you wouldn't let me kill you for $25 million. Yet, all have the same mathematical expectation.

Now, if we take this reasoning to its extreme, we get an interesting result — namely, that there is almost nothing for which it is worth taking even fairly small risks of dying. There are exceptions, and we will get to them in a minute. However, the point is that risking dying is like risking going broke in a poker tournament when you have a very good chance of winning if you can only survive for a while.

It certainly is true that if everybody thought like this, it would be harder to get people to fight and, thus, win a war. Politicians and generals do not analyze risking life the way that I just did. Or do they? Remember, the analysis assumed that it was your own life. I think that they would come to similar conclusions if it were their own life they were risking rather than yours.

There are times, however, when it is logically correct to risk your life. I will mention three:

1. When you are trying to prevent something even worse than death, such as torture or your child dying.
2. When you are trying to prevent something *almost* as bad as death, such as slavery, and the risks of dying are small.
3. When not taking the risk results in an even greater risk of dying for you or (if you want to be altruistic) for others.

It would seem that at least one, if not all, of these criteria was met as far as World War II was concerned. The risk of death, even our own, should not have deterred us in that case. The Civil War, on the other hand, can be justified only if it was about slavery, not if it was simply to prevent the South from seceding. (Can you imagine risking dying now to prevent the people of Montana from starting their own peaceful country if they desire. You wouldn't like it, but is it worth killing and dying to prevent it?) I have my doubts about World War I, the Korean War, and others, but I don't know enough about them. As far as Vietnam is concerned, an odd fact makes this war easier to judge. The fact of which I'm speaking is that we lost, and were thus not able to prevent whatever we would have prevented had we won. We can see the consequences of our loss by looking at Vietnam today, and can judge whether the soldiers who were taking maybe a 1 percent chance of dying were getting a fair risk vs. reward ratio. If we had won, Vietnam certainly would have been a little different than it is today, but would that difference have been worth more than 50,000 American lives?

# Legitimate Grievances

In the previous essay I had some things to say about war. The general thrust was that it is absurd to equate war to a game because people die, and the risk of dying cannot be analyzed in the same way as the risk of other losses, because the payoff is essentially minus infinity. Putting morality aside, the only ironclad reason to risk your life is if not doing so results in an even greater risk to your life (or results in something that you consider worse than death).

By this criteria, it does not seem that most wars are worth entering into. (On the other hand, those that are worth fighting are total struggles for survival — not games. It is ridiculous to have rules for war like the Geneva Convention rules. I believe that if you are forced to enter a war, you do whatever is necessary to keep your men from being killed, except possibly hurting enemy civilians.)

Now, what about those times when we have legitimate grievances of a serious nature but not serious enough to go to war by my criteria (see the previous essay). Is there any way to defuse the situation? One way that I can think of is best seen if we look at some incidents in the past that are logically similar to wars. I am speaking of duels — not sword fights, but prearranged face-offs usually with pistols. From what I understand, these duels would usually occur when one party challenged the other because of a perceived insult or grievance for which there was no rectification or apology. If the challenge was accepted, they would duel, and sometimes someone would die. What was odd about these duels (at least to me) was the strict rules that were set for them, and the fact that they were seen as a fight between two "gentlemen." However, a fight to the death between two gentlemen on a matter of honor is absurd. Here's why:

First of all, each party presumably believes that he is the one who is right in the dispute. In fact, if one party was clearly wrong, no one else such as "seconds" would be willing to become involved in a supposedly dignified duel, since there would be no honor in it.

The clearly guilty party could not achieve honor regardless of the outcome. However, one of the absurd things about duels is that the winner should never achieve any honor, except the honor of being the better shot! Whoever wins the duel does nothing to prove who was right in the dispute. He proves only who was the better dueler! That might be a reason to duel if you were sure that you were going to win, but don't bring honor or righteousness into it. (I'm always amazed when a dispute at the poker table results in two guys planning to "go outside" to settle it. That settles the dispute? Doesn't it just settle who is the better fighter? Also, what about the times when one person knowingly wrongs another but thinks that he can get out of it because he expects the other guy to foolishly challenge him. Rest assured that if I am knowingly wronged, I won't make this mistake. More on this shortly.)

There is a second, more important reason why duels don't make sense, however. That is the fact that you should not hate someone who thinks that he is right. You think that he has wronged you and that you are in the right, *but he thinks the opposite.* How do you know? *Because he is willing to risk his life to prove it.* In other words, the mere fact that he is willing to duel you means that you shouldn't. He thinks that he is right. No sane person would risk dying for any other reason. I think that you would agree that the intense hatred that will allow you to kill someone would at least partially dissipate if you knew that your adversary thought that he was in the right, even if he wasn't.

In the same way, I believe that we as a country should take notice anytime the people of another country would be willing to fervently fight and die to oppose us. It is possible that their government has misled them in the rightness of their cause — but can't the same be said for us?

I could end on that note, but I, instead, would like to use this opportunity to bring up one other illogical situation that occurs with many people. The best example is when a car cuts you off while driving. Do you get mad? Do you want revenge? Well, this makes no sense unless:

1. You would get equally mad if you saw that driver do it to someone else, or
2. He knows that it was you that he did it to.

Now, if you are honest with yourself, you will admit that you wouldn't be nearly as mad if you saw him cutting someone else off. It's only because he did it to you that makes you believe that you must show him that he can't get away with that. However, he doesn't know that it was you. So, if you need to show people that they shouldn't mess with you, save your wrath for those people who know that it was you with whom they messed.

# Some Short Thoughts

I have heard many arguments about whether John Wooden (former basketball coach of UCLA) was the best coach of all time. Many contend that he was. Some even go so far as to say that he was the best coach of any sport. Others say that he was a good coach, but far from the best, since he almost always had the best players. Wooden supporters admit this, but point out that the best team doesn't always win, yet Wooden managed to win about 80 percent of the end of the year tournaments. Tournaments in which he had to win at least four games in a row.

When someone is voted Manager or Coach of the Year in a particular sport, it is not always the coach of the championship team. Rather, it is the coach whose record is the best given the talent that he has to work with and the original expectation for his team. That seems to be a fair criteria, so how can we evaluate Wooden under this criteria when his typical team probably was in the neighborhood of a 3-to-1 favorite (on average) for each post-season game? He is expected to win, so how can he exceed expectation? Well, he couldn't in the regular season, even when his teams won 80 percent or better of their games. However, what about the tournament? Yes, he still was a 3-to-1 favorite per game even against these top teams, but he constantly won four or five in a row (when one loss would knock him out). The probability of this is $(¾)^4$ or $(¾)^5$. Before each tournament started, there was only a 20 percent to 30 percent chance that he would win it (most years), yet he constantly did. To win something like 10 out of 12 of these tournaments was, mathematically, almost 100,000-to-1! However, that is if UCLA was playing only its normally excellent game. It is much more reasonable to assume that Wooden was able to get his players to play far above even their own heads during the tournament, when it mattered, than to assume that a 100,000-to-1 shot came in. So, if your criteria for best coach is, in fact, how

179

much more he got out of his team than what was expected, no one beats John Wooden.

When you are talking silently to yourself, who is speaking and who is listening? I don't mean this as a joke. The point is that it seems unnecessary to say something to *yourself* since you already knew it ahead of time. When you tell your friend that you need an umbrella, it is so that he or she will know something that you already know, but why bother to say it to yourself? Yet this is how we perceive it to be when we think, "I need an umbrella." We hear ourselves saying it to ourselves even though we presumably knew it already! It's as if we are two people, and if we are, who is informing whom? None of the modern researchers on consciousness will satisfy me until they can answer this question.

Stores that advertise that they will automatically meet any competitor's price for the same item are not in the public good. This may be counterintuitive, but it is almost certainly true. One practical reason is that the store in question usually will charge fairly high prices, in general, for the unwary customer who assumes that he is getting the best price in town, but, in fact, isn't. The idea is to overcharge most customers who don't take you up on your offer (because they assume your offer implies that you normally have the lowest prices), while quickly dispensing with those few who do.

However, there is another more theoretical reason why the policy of matching all competitors' prices automatically is wrong and *probably should be outlawed.* In this country, the idea is that the free market mechanism will allow consumers to get the best products at the lowest prices. Competition does this. Competitors constantly are raising quality or lowering prices to entice customers. Collusion or price fixing among businesses is illegal, but a lowest-price guarantee policy indirectly does the same thing! Once one store does it, there is no incentive for its competitors to lower their prices. Now, in fact, all stores can raise their prices. This is because if a major store in the area has a well known price-guarantee policy, you can never steal business with a lower price. If I were a competitor of such a store, I actually might be happy it exists, as long as it keeps its prices high. Now, we both do better at the expense of the customer. This should be made illegal, if it isn't already under existing laws.

The argument that motorcycle helmets should not be mandatory is basically that people should have the freedom to choose to live dangerously if they desire. If they are willing to not ask the state to take care of them if they are hurt, the argument becomes powerful. However, those who try to use the same powerful argument to keep cigarettes legal are making a mistake. It is not the same argument, because unlike with helmets, those people who change their minds after their initial foray into danger cannot just as easily change their behavior. When you decide to start wearing a helmet, you just do it, but most cigarette smokers who decide to quit, don't just do it. They are hooked and got hooked, most likely, when they were too young to know better. It is this aspect of addiction, especially at a young age, that makes it different. This doesn't prove that cigarettes should be illegal, but the idea shouldn't make the libertarian cringe.

The daughter of a well-known gaming executive was kidnaped sometime ago. The mastermind was sentenced to 24 years. I think it should have been a bit less, not because he deserved less, but because *she didn't die.* We are not talking morality here, just simple logic. It probably would have irked the executive if the judge had said, "I sentence you to 15 years and, thus, a little hope, because you spared her life." However, suppose your child was kidnaped in Vegas a few months later? Wouldn't you have wanted such a statement from a judge to have made the news? It might be the difference of life and death for your child. More generally, all laws should have built into them some significant incentive for the criminal to spare lives. I agree that this at times can be repugnant, and that most criminals won't take these things into account when deciding whether or not to add murder to their crimes, but some will.

Should a basketball team that is losing by two points with a few seconds left go for a two-point or a three-point shot? If we assume that a three-point try has a 30 percent chance of being successful and a two-point try has a 50 percent chance, the answer is fairly clear cut. Your chance of winning is basically 30 percent if you go for the three points. If you go for the two points, you are even money to go into overtime. However, in overtime, you figure to be only about even money again. Thus, your chance of winning the game is only ¼, or 25 percent, if you go for the two points.

$$\frac{1}{4} = \left(\frac{1}{2}\right)\left(\frac{1}{2}\right)$$

The three-point shot with its 30 percent chance is almost definitely the better choice.

I recently read about a poor family that wouldn't accept welfare that struggled to barely make ends meet. All money went to food and shelter, none for fun. It occurred to me that businesses such as movie theaters, theme parks, and hotels have a few traits in common that could be relevant to these situations:

1. They operate on less than full capacity on their off-days.
2. It costs them little or nothing to accommodate extra patrons on these off days.
3. Giving customers a great deal like an 80 percent or 90 percent discount would cost them money only if some of those customers would have paid a higher price.

So, my idea is that the government and places like Disneyland, theaters, hotels, and so on, should start a program whereby people at the poverty level are given some sort of voucher that would allow them to take their kids to these places on non-busy days for just a few bucks. (Even these few bucks would be almost pure profit for businesses of this sort, especially since these people would never pay full price. However, I do not think that these programs should be absolutely free in order to avoid abuse.)

A few years ago, l read about a certain drug that was taken off the market. I forget what it treated. I do remember that it greatly helped about 40 percent of the patients who took it. The problem was that in a controlled study, in which half of the patients were taking a placebo sugar pill (but were told that they were taking the above-named medicine), 40 percent of the placebo takers also got better! The conclusion was that the drug was a scam, and that its total benefits came from the psychological "placebo effect" rather than from its chemical formula. The FDA thus had no choice but to take it off the market. However, keep in mind that placebos work only when the patient thinks that he is getting a real medicine. lf he knows that it is a placebo, there is no effect. Now my question is, what happened to the 40 percent of the sufferers who obtained relief? After the recall, did they go back to suffering? They couldn't just take a placebo. It seems absurd to suggest that a drug that has proven to be a fraud be kept on the market, but the alternative in this case seemed worse yet. If fooling the brain can make some people better, maybe we should do it. The current controversy about allowing marijuana for cancer patients might be a good example.

# Some More Short Thoughts

Here's a bunch of short thoughts that I think are hard to refute.

With 100 different religions believing 100 different things the number of religions that believe something that is incorrect may be all 100 but is at least 99.

Have you ever noticed that debris in the middle of the freeway is almost always on the lines between the lanes? Hopefully, you understand that this isn't a cosmic coincidence, but rather caused by the fact that the debris is jostled back and forth by passing cars until it randomly reaches a spot where it won't be jostled anymore. And this is where it stays. Similarly if you notice that most poker machine junkies play close to perfect strategy you should not assume that they have studied the books. More likely they are one of the few who hit upon a good strategy by chance. With so many prospective addicts out there a few will just so happen to play well but they are the ones you usually see as the others quickly go broke. (Of course these are simply two examples of a general principle that applies to many things including of course the theory of evolution.)

If two equal players are playing a freezeout and one player has X dollars and the other has Y dollars it is simple to prove that the chances of winning are exactly in proportion to the ratio on the money. If it wasn't so, then one of the two players would be expected to be ahead after multiple freezeouts, but we already said that the players are equal. It is not true that the shorter stack has an advantage. That is only so when there are more than two players involved. Think about it.

185

A very small difference among average values can turn into a big difference in the "tails" of the normal distribution. For instance: If the average 100 yard dash for a guy with dark hair is 12.3 seconds, and a redhead is 12.1 seconds, then a random dark haired guy is maybe 45 percent likelier to beat a random redhead in a race. But if I knew the winner broke 10 seconds flat, I could probably lay 5-to-1 odds that it was the redhead that won. (It is for this reason that people form stereotypes when there is only a modicum of truth to them.)

When the airlines were not forced to provide special seats for young children some people suggested that that was good enough reason to stop flying. What about the fact that switching to a car makes your children about 50 times more likely to get killed?

For those of you who are wondering what you will feel like in the year 2200, just remember what it was like in 1800. You were dead then too. (Actually, there is another possibility. See the last chapter.)

♣ ♦ ♥ ♠

Even a subject as controversial as abortion has aspects to it that are reducible to logic or at least logical consistency. By that I mean if you believe "A" then you must believe "B." As an example, suppose you believe that artificial birth control is OK, but that abortion isn't. Presumably you believe this because you think it is not wrong to prevent a *potential* human being (by stopping sperm from reaching an egg) but feel differently once the egg is fertilized. At this point you believe there is a specific person (a specific "soul?") that should not be terminated. For those who feel this way it should be pointed out that there is a difference between a two month old embryo and a two day old fertilized egg. The fertilized egg is not destined to become a specific human being until quite a few days after fertilization. Before that you can do many things to the splitting of the egg and get many results. Nature herself can split the egg into twins, triplets, etc.

So stopping a one day old fertilized egg from developing is logically just about the same as stopping a specific sperm from hitting an egg. Specifically, this means that those of you who accept birth control but not abortion should be able to accept the "abortion pill" if it is used soon enough after conception.

# Crime and Punishment

Poker is analogous to real life in a number of areas, not the least of which is crime and punishment. And if you analyze certain aspects of criminal justice using poker logic, you'll come to some interesting and surprising conclusions.

Why do we throw criminals in jail? There appear to he three primary reasons.

1. To deter them or others from committing that particular crime.
2. To keep a dangerous person off the streets.
3. To satisfy society's and/or the victim's need for justice.

In most cases when a convicted person is sent to prison it is for all of the above reasons. But not always. For instance, serial killers are sent away mainly for reasons 2 and 3. We know that nuts like this usually cannot he deterred by the threat of jail (or even execution). On the other hand, nonviolent white-collar criminals go to jail mainly for reason number one.

So let us look at the concept of deterrence a little more closely. First, we'll need to accept the given that the whole subject of determining appropriate punishment comes up because there are bad people out there. My mother would never commit a major crime even if she knew nothing would happen to her if she did, and neither would yours. So the existence of punishment does nothing to stop people like her. She doesn't need the deterrent.

On the other side of the coin are those people who have a screw loose and commit their crimes with little or no regard for the consequences. Punishment doesn't deter them either.

The truth is that punishment is only a strong deterrent for those immoral people who look at life and other people as if they were in a poker game. So as to the question of committing a crime, they would simply evaluate the risk versus reward much as a poker player would when contemplating "stealing" a pot.

Consider this simple example: Suppose Joe X knows he has a 95 percent chance of getting away with lying on his income tax form. If he pulls it off he would save $2,000. If not, the fine would be $10,000. Mathematically, the reward justifies the risk if right and wrong are removed from the equation. So an immoral person is apt to commit this crime.

To stop him you would theoretically have to increase the fine to about $40,000 or increase the chances of getting caught to about 20 percent. The idea applies to more serious crimes as well. Suppose someone decides that he would be willing to spend three years in jail for a million dollars (or that he would pay no more than a million dollars to avoid three years in jail). Mathematically this means that it would be worth committing a burglary netting a $150,000 "score" if there were only a 10 percent chance of getting caught. The analytical criminal mind would come to the same conclusion. To change the equation to the point where a criminal wouldn't commit the crime there would have to be either: (1) less money to be gained; (2) a longer jail sentence (or some other punishment that he wouldn't want to suffer for a million dollars); (3) a higher probability of getting caught.

To balance the risks versus rewards in the minds of the criminally-inclined, I think we can make some observations and suggestions:

1. When deciding on an appropriate punishment for a crime (especially one that involves money) the severity of the crime should not be all that is considered. The court system should also take into account the *probability of getting caught*. While this is not always easy to judge, the fact remains that some crimes are much easier to get away with than others. To keep such crimes from becoming "good plays" in the criminal's mind, the punishment must be more severe even if the crime itself is no more heinous than others where it's easier to be caught. If this results in especially

severe punishments that are deemed unconstitutional, amend the constitution.

2. When selecting punishment that is effective in deterring analytical would-be criminals who weigh risk versus reward, it is not necessary that jail be used as a deterrent. Anything that will make the crime no longer a "good play" will do. The punishment might be cutting off their hand, or making the criminal sing the national anthem on live TV before the Super Bowl. Prisons should be used mainly for violent people who must be locked up. If other equally effective deterrent punishments for nonviolent criminals are unconstitutional, amend the constitution.

3. We should realize that those criminals who commit crimes that are clearly "bad plays" (by the poker risk vs. reward criteria) are more sick than evil. The truly evil person is the one who would, for instance, rape women were it not for the punishment he fears. (And the fact that there are men like this out there is demonstrated periodically when there is a conquering army and some of the soldiers take advantage of the fact that they can rape with impunity.) Those who rape anyway, in spite of the obvious probable severe consequences, may need to be put away but probably shouldn't be reviled. *Rather those who walk among us who are law abiding only because of the consequences of crime are the ones to be considered the most despicable* (as well as those few in prison who got unlucky while committing a "good play" crime).

4. Expanding on the above thought as it might apply to capital punishment: Even proponents of the death penalty usually agree that it should be applied only to the most evil criminals. This is especially the case if they can be sure that all dangerous murderers who are not executed are truly locked up for life. But following the logic I've used so far, it must be apparent that the only clearly evil murderers are the ones who committed their crimes after coolly evaluating whether the gain justified the risk — people, in other words, who would have refrained from murder if they thought there

was less to gain or if they thought the chances of getting caught were great. The most obvious examples of this type of criminal are hired hit men. (And those who hired them.) Other examples are any other type of organized crime killers as well as those who kill to collect insurance or to silence a prospective witness to another crime. These criminals should be executed if not tortured.

But I have a problem with taking the life of someone who is not this logically evil. Executing a person who kills when it is clearly irrational to do so is like killing a wild animal. This person is sick, not evil: executing such a person can only be justified for public safety reasons, not moral reasons. Ironically this concept would apply most strongly to the most revolting killers, like Jeffrey Dahmer or Leonard Lake, men who couldn't possibly have been coldly calculating risk versus reward.

# Game Theory, Logic, Crime and Punishment

Note: This essay repeats many of the ideas of the previous one but has some other ideas as well.

Consider three types of people with respect to economic crime. There are those who would never commit an economic crime whether they could get away with it or not. There are those who feel that their only hope is crime and don't worry about the consequences. And there are those who do not steal money only because of the consequences. Obviously, it is mainly for this third type that we have punishment at all.

Punishment, whether it be prison, a fine, or enforced community service, is the reason people of this third type will not steal, not a sense of right and wrong. For them the decision about whether or not to commit a crime is based solely on weighing the pros and cons, not morality. Thus, the punishment for committing a particular crime must be great enough so that it is not a "good play."

An analogy arises from poker. To decide whether to bluff (steal) a pot one analyzes the risks versus the rewards. Specifically, one notes what a successful bluff will win when it works (the money in the pot), compares this to what it will cost when it doesn't (the size of the bluff) and then calculates what to do after considering the likelihood of success. All factors need to be evaluated.

Similar results can be used if you are cold-bloodedly evaluating whether or not committing a crime is a good play. What you do in essence is divide the amount of money you will gain if "successful" by the chance of getting caught and compare this mathematical expectation with the penalty if caught. If the penalty is other than a fine, you would have to assign your own monetary value to the sentence. As an example, if burglarizing a house will net you an expected $50,000 or a one year jail sentence, and that one year in jail is something you would have to be paid $400,000 to endure, then the crime is mathematically a good play if there is less than a one in nine chance of getting caught.

If deterrence is to be the objective of criminal sentences for non-violent economic crimes, then they must be severe enough to keep the crimes from being a good play. Many lawmakers and judges are already partially aware of this concept. However most do not realize that in order to determine the punishment necessary to keep a crime from being a good play, it is necessary to take into account the chance of being caught and convicted for that particular crime.

To have equal degrees of deterrence for crimes involving the same amount of money, you must have greater penalties for those crimes that are easier to get away with! Since the chances of success are part of the criminal's calculations, they should also be part of the judge's and the lawmaker's. For the most part they are not.

Simply stated, many punishments assigned to many crimes are illogical or inconsistent with society's own principles. There are generally four main reasons why we punish people who commit crimes. These are:

1. Public safety
2. Deterrence
3. Rehabilitation
4. Punishment

*Public safety* is obviously a good reason to lock up criminals, especially violent ones who, if not incarcerated, might strike again. Rapists and child molesters are not usually deterred by the threat of prison. However, we put them in prison to keep them away from us. (Nonetheless, people like these should not be utterly despised. Anyone who commits a crime that is clearly a "bad play" in the mathematical sense previously discussed must have problems beyond their control.)

*Deterrence* is clearly a good reason for punishment as it actually does stop crime. Some people, who can control themselves, would commit crimes were it not for the punishment. However, they will only commit crimes that in their judgement are good plays. Then it is not necessary that they be locked up for public safety reasons as long as other punishments have equal deterrence value for them.

*Rehabilitation* would be a good reason to send people to prison if in fact the prison did rehabilitate. The fact that it usually does just the opposite eliminates this reason from further discussion.

*Pure punishment* is the fourth reason we lock people up. Many think that people who commit a major crime should go to prison even if there is no chance they will do it again and even if it will not deter others from doing it. Others say society as a whole does not need pure revenge but should only be concerned with protecting itself from future crime.

Judges would do well to cite which of these four reasons determined the sentences they "assign." For instance, when sentencing a counterfeiter, the judge might say something like, "You get 10 years, not because you are a danger to society, but rather to keep others from thinking that the eventual punishment for a crime of this nature is so lenient that the rewards are worth the risk." To a child molester the judge might say, "Your sentence may not deter others from this crime, but it will keep you off the streets."

An example of an illogical sentence is the one for attempted murder. Should one get a significantly lighter sentence because he or she is a bad shot? The criminal tries to kill, but the victim is saved by modern medicine. If the victim had died it would be murder and the punishment would be quite a bit more severe. This makes no sense. From the standpoint of public safety the criminal is just as dangerous whether the victim lives or dies. From the standpoint of deterrence, the same is true.

After all, society is equally intent on deterring attempted murder as well as murder since it is just a matter of luck as to which crime was actually committed. Even with respect to pure punishment, can it be said that the criminal deserved a lesser sentence because the victim got lucky and lived? Pure luck should never be a factor when evaluating crime and punishment.

Is it not the same with respect to drunk driving? A very drunk driver should consider himself lucky if he *doesn't* kill somebody. Why should the punishment be that much different when he does? (I do suggest that there should be a more severe punishment for driving while *very* drunk, rather than lumping everyone together who is driving with a blood alcohol level above a certain amount. The higher the level, the worse the crime.)

Consider this. If a person is imprisoned only for reasons of deterrence or punishment and there are no public safety considerations, why not let him out of prison while keeping the punishment just as severe? How? Not with 1,000 hours of community service but rather with something like continual long term menial but necessary work — such as cleaning subway stations. With prisons as over populated as they are now, many criminals are being released simply because of overcrowding. The logical solution would be to keep the dangerous ones locked up and punish the others in ways that are just as objectionable to them, but might accomplish something for society, as well.

What about those criminal defendants who seem obviously guilty but are acquitted because the jury was not *absolutely* certain of their guilt, or the incriminating evidence was obtained without a search warrant, or some such technicality?[10] In this country those on trial are "innocent until proven guilty." And they are found innocent unless the jury unanimously considers them "guilty beyond a reasonable doubt." This is a good system, but it could be made better. Also, the system has some serious implications that most people do not understand.

For instance, there is a lack of precision in the expression "reasonable doubt." Doesn't it make more sense to create a specific probability of guilt as the criteria for jurors? For example, a juror could be instructed to vote for acquittal if he or she thought the probability of the accused being innocent was greater than five

---

[10]This essay was originally written well before the OJ Simpson trial. The idea you are about to read about seemed farfetched at the time. OJ may have changed that.

percent. No doubt it would be hard to quantify an opinion as to guilt or innocence, but some guidelines about the certainty of guilt before voting for conviction are better than no guidelines at all. Even without a specific numerical guideline, most jurors will vote to acquit unless they perceive a high probability that the accused is actually guilty.

When a jury returns a verdict, four different results are possible:

1. They can convict a guilty man/woman.
2. They can acquit an innocent man/woman.
3. They can convict an innocent man/woman.
4. They can acquit a guilty man/woman.

The last two possibilities are obviously errors. Statisticians separate these two errors into what they call Type I and Type II errors. And they have proven that the less likely you are to make a Type I error, the more likely you are to make a Type II error, and vice versa. In other words, if you set up an experiment where it is imperative that you make very few Type I errors, you can expect to make a lot of Type II errors.

Since trials in this country are set up so as to avoid at almost all costs the tragedy of convicting an innocent person, it necessarily follows that many guilty people will be set free. Therefore, we need another way the jury can vote that is in between innocent and guilty. It could be called "probably guilty." This verdict could be returned if the jury was less than certain of guilt, but still felt the guilt was very likely. The verdict of probably guilty could also be returned in those cases where guilt is obvious, but the defendant would have ordinarily have been acquitted because of a technicality.

Probably guilty is a verdict that should be available only in the case of major crimes. For those receiving this verdict, there should be no incarceration. However, those found guilty should lose some of their rights for a period of time. They should be kept under surveillance for the public safety, be subject to search, and be kept from certain jobs. After all, does it make sense that a child molester who gets off on a technicality should be able to use constitutional rights to make it easier for him to strike again?

For major crimes the jury should convict if they are certain of guilt beyond a reasonable doubt, but should be allowed to return a probably guilty verdict if they are let's say, 80 percent certain of guilt, or if a technicality doesn't allow them to convict. (However, even a verdict of probably guilty should not be allowed in the case of gross police misconduct. Otherwise law enforcement officials might be tempted to use illegal means to obtain evidence in otherwise tough cases expecting a probably guilty verdict for their efforts.) Those found probably guilty would find themselves in a situation similar to people on probation or parole.

What of capital cases? Unfortunately, we have to allow juries to convict defendants when they think there is a very slight, say one percent, chance that they are innocent. To do otherwise would allow too many killers to go free. However, the idea of a significant number of executions of innocent people is so repugnant, special care must be taken to avoid such errors. When the death sentence is involved we need another possible verdict, "guilt beyond a shadow of a doubt."

This verdict would reflect an even greater degree of certainty than a simple guilty verdict, which in effect says, guilty beyond a reasonable doubt. A simple guilty verdict would limit the sentence to a maximum of life imprisonment. At present, the judge or jury, after finding a defendant guilty of a capital crime, often goes on to decide whether to impose the death sentence. This decision is usually based on the number of mitigating circumstances, the brutality of the crime, the defendant's criminal history and so forth. *But another mitigating factor should be whether there is the slightest degree of doubt as to the actual guilt of the defendant.* Even if this doubt is not sufficient to prevent a guilty verdict, it should be enough to save someone's life.

The foregoing has only touched on how the criminal justice system could be changed for the better by simple logic. For instance to blindly announce that an acquitted defendant is simply not guilty when we know that there is still a good probability that he is, is to close our eyes to the truth. Determining guilt or innocence is an inexact process. Surely the concept of probability should come into play in the process, especially where violent crimes are concerned.

Determination of punishment should likewise be put on a more logical basis. All factors should be analyzed including what we are trying to accomplish for society with this punishment and what the probability is that the criminal could have gotten away with his crime. At present only the severity of the crime and the defendant's past record are taken into account when determining sentences.

Our entire criminal justice system should be put on a more scientific basis. To do this we must make greater use of logic, we must see the truth as it is rather than as we would like it to be, and we must more often apply the science of probability. We have nothing to lose but a badly out moded, dangerously ineffective, and overly expensive criminal justice system in America.

# Diversity

One of the first things that strikes you when you walk into any of the Southern California poker casinos is the wide diversity of racial and ethnic backgrounds among both customers (players) and employees. Overall I would estimate that of the two or three thousand people in the room, 30 percent are white, 30 percent Asian, 15 percent black, 10 percent middle-eastern, 10 percent Hispanic, and 5 percent are who knows what. (These figures would vary somewhat depending on which casino you were talking about.)

Furthermore the Asian contingent can be broken down into Chinese, Japanese, Korean, Vietnamese, and other Southeast Asians — people who have historically not always gotten along. But the fact is that in the cardroom setting they and all the other races get along splendidly. Not just the Asians, but everyone.

In twenty years of playing poker in California cardrooms, I have seen very few fights and have never seen a fight with racial overtones. I have never even heard an ethnic slur, except for a few obviously said in jest. This fact was so striking to me that I actually recently sent a letter to President Clinton suggesting that he visit the Commerce, Bicycle, Normandie, or Hollywood Park Casinos where he could witness this phenomenon firsthand. I pointed out in the letter that there was probably no place else on earth other than these card clubs that so well illustrated an important principle of human relations — one I'll get to in a moment.

There are a few other places where two or more racial or ethnic groups work in harmony. Professional sports teams, for instance. But besides the fact that there are far fewer people involved, the difference in sports is that in that workplace everyone is helping each other make money. Naturally, in those circumstances, people will be friendly and cooperate, even if deep down they don't like each other.

But in a card casino everyone is trying to *take* each other's money. You would think this would make card casinos a powder keg, especially if you believe that many people harbor animosity to others of a different race. But this clearly has not been the case, even when there are thousands of people in the cardrooms, any two of whom could start a fight.

So I got to thinking. Why is it that there are never any racial incidents or even real animosity among all these disparate people, even in this highly charged competitive atmosphere where everyone is struggling (sometimes desperately) to win or at least not to lose to people who are trying to take their money?

Though this is not a pure math or logic question, I'm sure I have the answer. And it is not that these casinos have tough and efficient security, although they do. Rather it is because everyone knows that they will be treated fairly and equally. If you lose your money to someone else it is because of his or her cards, not his or her skin color. It is even okay to lose to an opponent of another ethnicity because that opponent plays better — as long as you know that you figure to win if you play better.

In other words, I believe the important principle that is illustrated so well and so uniquely by the California card clubs is this: Racial bitterness stems mainly from the perception of unfair treatment when that treatment is because of race. These casinos show that all different kinds of people will accept coming in second if the reason is truly skill or merit. Or even luck in the short run. Just give everybody a fair shake. The same fair shake.

# Solving The
# Race Relation Problem

For this essay I thought that I would address something simple, namely solving the race relation problem. As with many subjects there is a mathematical aspect to it that people do not see.

One of the aftermaths of the O.J. Simpson trial was the large difference of opinion between blacks and whites as to how likely it would be that the police would plant evidence on a black man. Many African-Americans thought this highly plausible given their day to day experiences. These experiences told them that a high proportion of white people are racist, not just cops. Many white people, on the other hand, especially those who considered themselves not racist thought this was silly.

Now in a moment I am going to explain what is actually going on here. Hopefully this will help people understand the other's viewpoints and get along better. First, let's make sure we all agree on the definition of racism. I think it means to label, dislike, and mistrust someone simply because of his or her race regardless of what kind of person they are.

The strange thing is that even if we all agree on this definition, there are many white people who would say they are not racist while black people would say they are. This is true because there are many white people who in their hearts and minds feel they are not racists but *their actions say otherwise.* I am talking about little things here. The way a white person may act when an African-American gets into the elevator with him or her, or a fleeting look of surprise when coming upon a black neurosurgeon or airline pilot. Black people take these things as signs of racism. To them it is usually racism when the white person says or does something different than he would if he were only in the presence of whites. And it is easy to see their point. After all even these small distinctions are *illegal* to make if you are talking about hiring someone or serving someone. The law says that public companies should judge people solely on the basis of what kind of person they are. Why shouldn't individual people be held to this same standard? Yet individual people, even those who claim not to be racist do not always act that nobly. African-Americans see this and are justifiably upset even if they suspect that the white persons action may be done subconsciously. And it seems that blacks are singled out for their (conscious or subconscious) unfair treatment much more than the ethnic groups. White people should realize this and be more empathetic.

However, African-Americans should also be a bit more understanding. This is where mathematics and logic comes in. They must realize that part of the problem arises from two undeniable facts, one permanent; one temporary. The first fact is that black people are *instantly identifiable*. This is not true for most other ethnic groups. Now if you are a member of a group that is instantly identifiable this is a bad break for you if there are negative feelings toward some members of that group. You are subconsciously instantly labeled before you have a chance to prove yourself as a person. The second (this time temporary) fact is that a slightly higher percentage of black people (in this country) tend to be "trouble" or "unqualified." I have little doubt that this fact is because of past injustice and will not always be true. (Affirmative action may speed the process.) Furthermore, the numbers are small. Maybe 2 percent of white people and 3 percent of African-Americans are "trouble makers." Still the question is does a white person (or black person for that matter) have a right to take this small statistical difference into account when he has nothing else to go on. The answer is certainly no if you are the personnel director of a company. Even if there was some statistical correlation between the race of your applicants and their chances of doing a good job, you have time to test and interview everybody and make a decision based on those more accurate factors.

But the same is not true for an individual in a spur of the moment decision. Statistical factors come into play. It is hard to ask someone to ignore a statistical factor that is staring him in the face even if that means he is probably slighting a good upstanding individual who has similar physical characteristics to a very small group of "bad apples."

It is important to understand what I am saying here. It is that I would hope African-Americans would give white people a little bit of a break for "playing the odds" (usually subconsciously) as unfair as that may be. They should of course give them that break only in those spur of the moment situations. But I really think a bit of understanding will get things fixed faster than if a big deal is made out of a mathematical fact of life.

# An Unexpected Ending

Pretend that you are living in the 23rd century. Now I would like you to consider the following hypothetical scenario. You have some kind of horrible accident that leaves you completely paralyzed. Medical science has still not found a way to cure this. You have no close friends or family that you can expect to visit you in the hospital. Things look bleak. You have no desire to spend your days in a wheelchair that you control with your eyelids. However, there is an alternative. It involves going to a special hospital built just for cases like yours. This is what you choose.

When you first arrive at the hospital you are put into a room that has a TV directly over the bed staring down at you. You are aware of your surroundings but your attention is mainly on the TV. After all you can't get much enjoyment from the real world. In a few days the hospital staff shuts out the real world completely. They do this by fitting to your head something similar to goggles. The TV show is broadcast to the inside of each lens. (Such things exist even now.) Since you are totally paralyzed you are now completely unaware of anything except what you see and hear on TV. Doctors are still attending to you and you are being fed intravenously but you can't tell.

Once the hospital staff has seen that you have adjusted to the goggles and your new state of affairs, they take you to the next step. That is they disconnect your goggles from the commercial TV station and instead connect it to a closed circuit TV camera and microphone. But this TV camera is mounted on a robot that can move around. Furthermore what makes the robot move are your brain waves! (Please understand that this is not at all farfetched. Brain activity is simply electricity and even today we have some simple devices that can be made to move or work by a person's thoughts when his brain waves are suitably connected to the device.)

So we have this robot that can move around following your thought commands (just as your real body once did) and the hospital staff puts it out in the real world, preferably your hometown. Lo and behold you can once again see and hear things outside your hospital bed. When people encounter your robot on the street they will know that if they speak to it or show it something, they are really speaking and dealing with you (or at least some person in a hospital bed). So you can see people, enjoy a sunset or even watch TV by planting your robot in front of a set.

Now as years go by various technical improvements are made to your robot. The first one is the addition of a voice synthesizer that is connected to the language center of your brain. It's done in such a way that when you think of words the robot speaks them. (We are now beyond our present technology but I don't think by much.) Now you can really interact with people from the outside world since you can talk to them! And when your robot happens to come upon another comparably equipped robot, your robot can have a conversation with it. Of course we know that it is really one paralyzed person talking to another paralyzed person.

The next step is to make the robots more human looking and to add the other three senses; taste, touch, and smell. Now you can live an almost normal life. Though you are lying in bed, you are barely aware of it. You live life through your robot. If you have your robot eat food, *you* taste it. If you have your robot patronize a massage parlor *you* feel it. If there are male and female robots you can even make love. The bottom line is that your robot can become a regular member of the community even though everybody knows that it is really you and your thoughts and desires that they are dealing with when they are interacting with your robot.

At this point it becomes not at all uncommon to see a robot walking down the street. After all, the technology is so wonderful that it is offered to all paralyzed people. But a problem arises. Though robots look fairly similar to human beings they are different and this makes some people uncomfortable. So a proposal is made that since there are so many of these robots around why not just set aside a special place for only them. Let them interact with each other. And the proposal is enacted.

All of the robots including yours are shipped off to another place, maybe an island, maybe another planet, maybe even another dimension. Still it's not so bad. Your only companions are now other robots but *they* are connected to real people just as yours is. And you can do basically the same things you could do before your accident and enjoy these things almost as much; This is especially true if you can forget about the fact that you are really lying in a hospital bed as are all your new found friends (and lovers?). Which is why a few years later, on one particular night a group of human do gooders, sneak into all of the hospital rooms around the world that contain paralyzed people attached to robots. They then proceed to give all these patients including you an injection. This injection puts you to sleep for a while after which you wake up with a permanent case of full fledged amnesia!

So what do you think when you wake up? That is a tough question. But one thing is for sure; you don't know that you are really lying in a hospital bed. When your robot touches its face you feel it but you have no idea that "you" aren't right there in robot land. There is no way for you to tell that the seat of your consciousness is thousands or millions of miles away or in another dimension. The same goes for all the other robots. If you think about it you will understand that there really is no way to tell that "you" are not your robot. But I take that back because there *is* one way to tell. Suppose one day after this mass amnesia inducing incident, another robot chases your robot with an axe. You try to get away but you fail. As the axe comes arcing towards your robot's "head" you say to yourself "I am about to die." When the axe finds its mark everything goes black; No sights, no sounds, no smells, or anything else. After all your destroyed robot was your only link to the outside world. But there is something strange. You can still *think*. Somehow you are not really dead. And of course you are not. But notice that there was no way that you could realize this until the robot that you thought was "you" no longer existed as a viable entity. Your robot had to "die" before you could understand how you live on.

Now wouldn't it be nice if your body was merely a robot like the one in this story rather than being the real you? But wait a second. How do you know that it's not?